INDEX ON CENSORSHIP 4 1997

Volume 26 No 4 July/August 1997 Issue 177

Editor & Chief Executive
Ursula Owen

Deputy Editor
Judith Vidal-Hall

News Editor
Sarah A Smith

Production Editor
Rose Bell

Eastern Europe Editor
Irena Maryniak

Editorial Co-ordinator
Nevine Mabro

Fundraising Manager
Elizabeth Twining

Fundraising Executive
Joe Hipgrave

Circulation & Marketing Director
Louise Tyson

Subscriptions
Syra Morley

Office Manager
Gary Netherton

Website Manager
Jules Nurrish

Volunteer Assistants
William Asampong
Jessie Banfield
Michaela Becker
Penny Dale
Victoria Millar
Philippa Nugent
William Ocaya
Briony Stocker
Tara Warren
Darryl Wilks

Cover design by Senate
Front cover: Oil derricks,
Baku, Azerbaijan ©John
Spaull/Panos Pictures
Back cover: Detail from
1980s revolutionary mural
in Tehran, Iran ©Kaveh
Golestan

Index on Censorship (ISSN 0306-4220) is published bi-monthly by a non-profit-making company: Writers & Scholars International Ltd, Lancaster House, 33 Islington High Street, London N1 9LH *Tel*: 0171-278 2313 *Fax*: 0171-278 1878 *Email*: indexoncenso@gn.apc.org http://www.oneworld.org/index_oc/ *Index on Censorship* is associated with Writers & Scholars Educational Trust, registered charity number 325003
Periodicals postage: (US subscribers only) paid at Newark, New Jersey. Postmaster: send US address changes to *Index on Censorship* c/o Mercury Airfreight Int/ Ltd Inc, 2323 Randolph Avenue, Avenel, NJ 07001, USA

Subscriptions 1997 (6 issues p.a.) Individuals: UK £38, US $50, rest of world £43 Institutions: UK £42, US $72, rest of world £48 Students: UK £25, US $35, rest of world £31

Index on Censorship and Writers and Scholars Educational Trust
depend on donations to guarantee their independence and to fund research
The Trustees and Directors would like to thank all those whose
donations support Index and WSET, including

The Bromley Trust
David Hockney (sale of donated print)
The Lyndhurst Settlement
The Ruben and Elisabeth Rausing Trust

Former Editors: Michael Scammell (1972-81); Hugh Lunghi (1981-83); George Theiner (1983-88); Sally Laird (1988-89); Andrew Graham-Yooll (1989-93)

EDITORIAL

Who has the power?

'THE drive is commercial, the role is commercial and what we do is commercial.' John Jennings, chairman of Shell International Transport and Trading, in an issue of *Index* devoted to oil and human rights implies that, though Shell (which owns or leases about 400 million acres of land worldwide) might state their concerns for indigenous populations, it is commercial decisions which dictate policy.

The romantic view of oil — its early contribution to light and heat, to industrialisation, the creation of business empires and mergers, even eventually soap operas — is over. Today, as Edward Morse writes, the industry tends to be associated with enormous profits, environmental damage, human rights violations, global warming and war. Questions have been asked about the nature of Shell's involvement in Nigeria, about BP's alleged connections with the Colombian military, said to have murdered protesters against environmental degradation. More than that, there has been a huge transfer of power in the global trading system, as John Vidal has written in the *Guardian*, from governments to corporations. With the annual value of world oil more than the annual gross domestic product of any country outside the G7, the oil industry is now so powerful that one has to ask — who calls the tune?

And where does such a scenario leave democracy and human rights? The arguments over where the oil pipelines from the Caspian region (due to become the largest source of oil after the Middle East) will go are, as Olivier Roy and Irena Maryniak make clear, fundamentally political and strategic, rather than concerned with the well-being of its population. Already suffering from the effects of civil wars which have cut deeply into the fabric of their daily life (even journalists in this region find it hard to disentangle themselves from distorting loyalties), the people find it well-nigh impossible to discover what is being decided in their name.

Given the reality of the power balance — social accountability not high on the agenda of oil companies and national governments increasingly forced to kowtow to them — is it not perhaps to the corporations that we should be addressing our concerns? This is the first of several issues of *Index* which will look at who actually has power over people's civil and human rights, and what the implications are of demands for change. ❑

contents

TWENTY FIVE YEARS OF INDEX

Among those celebrating *Index*'s 25 years of publication at the Delfina Studio in London on 22 May 1997:

Founder supporters Tom Stoppard, Lois Sieff, Jim Rose, Natasha Spender, Stuart Hampshire (above)

Banned Chinese poet Yang Lian (left)

Milen Radev presenting a 25th birthday cartoon to chairman Sue Woodford (below, left)

Ursula Owen, Louise Tyson, Ariel Dorfman (below)

Our thanks to Lord Palumbo, Waterstones and the Delfina Studio for supporting the event.
Photographs © Susan Greenhill

Hong Kong — the shape of things to come

• **But is it art?** On 20 May Hong Kong's Urban Council rejected the Hong Kong Alliance in Support of Democratic Movement in China's request to display a statue commemorating the 1989 Tiananmen Square massacre in a local park from June to September. Though with little artistic merit and a fairly crude political message, the sculpture, which is known as the 'Pillar of Shame', was, nevertheless, turned down as a 'political work of art'.

• **Bias binding** In early June staff at a Kowloon technical institute were warned against encouraging students to take part in political activities and criticised for the political 'bias' of their civic education programme. Posters commemorating the Tiananmen Square massacre were banned from the school.

• **Turned turtle** Around the same time, a survey in the *South China Morning Post* found that three out of five message-paging firms examined refused to take messages deemed offensive to China's premier, Li Peng. The term they were quizzed on — 'turtle's egg' — a common Chinese insult, is the equivalent of the familiar and innocuous usage — even by members of the UK parliament — of 'bastard' in English.

• **Happy times are here again** However, in the euphoria of the 1 July return to the motherland, these were minor matters. According to a survey carried out by the *Los Angeles Times*, more than 60 per cent of

Hong Kong residents unsurprisingly expressed themselves well content with the handover and optimistic about the future.

• **Record breakers** As was demonstrated by the unprecedented turnout at the colony's final meeting of the Hong Kong Jockey Club on 15 June. No-one, it seemed, cared that the erstwhile 'Royal' gathering would be 'People's' by its next meeting, and a record crowd of 88,000 contributed HK$2.8 billion — another record — to the tote's turnover. Since gambling has been officially banned in the People's Republic since 1949, Hong Kong will be the only legitimate outlet for the Chinese addiction to gambling after 1 July. But since hypocrisy is the name of the game in Beijing when it comes to individual enterprise across the mahjong tiles or over a card table, and the Party has proved unequal to the task of curbing the mainland mania, they have hedged their bets by promising to keep the Hong Kong racetrack open. Not only have the enterprising scions of Beijing's mandarins already inserted themselves in its management, but it is a healthy contributor to charitable and social service revenues too. In Hong Kong, they are already laying odds that the first meeting of the new era will even break the records achieved under the *ancien régime*.

• **Joy confined** Ironically — but equally unsurprisingly — residents of Beijing are showing a lot less enthusiasm for the great day than their soon-to-be-compatriots in Hong Kong. There is a distinct lack of that joyful celebration exhorted by the authorities at this momentous juncture in China's long history. Not that they are being given much room to express any feelings on the occasion. Beijing is under a state of military siege comparable to the martial law imposed during the Tiananmen demonstrations of 1989. The square itself is completely cut off and the army is out in force. The government, it seems, fears its people may misconstrue the official invitation to gather and make merry as China's historic 'page of shame' is finally expunged from memory.

• **Reversal of fortune** But, at the same time, and not to be overlooked, the end of May saw the first reversal of verdicts on Tiananmen Square dissidents. Leng Wanbao, on medical parole since 1994, heard that his conviction for organising a 'counter-revolutionary clique' had been overturned. His co-defendants Tang Yuanjuan and Li Wei were released on 9 June. ❑

Yesterday's headlines... Today's headlines... Tomorrow's headlines?

• **No laughing matter** Zimbabwe's President Robert Mugabe is having a difficult summer. A cartoon in the *Zimbabwe Independent* on 23 May suggesting Mugabe could be the next African ruler to follow Zaire's Mobuto Sese Seko into exile, naturally ruffled feathers in high places. Rather than ignoring a not particularly biting piece of satire, minister of information and tourism, Joyce Mujuru, described Tony Namate's cartoons as 'treasonable, infuriating, unacceptable' and says she will sue Namate on behalf of the state.

• **Kissing with confidence** Prohibitions on public displays of affection caused passions to rise in two very different parts of the world this summer. Sicilian Mayor Salvino Caputo was pressurised to withdraw his ban on kissing in the main town square of Monreale when local youths organised a protest 'kiss-in' on 19 June. Iranian film director Abbas Kiarostami, however, suffered condemnation for kisses exchanged with Catherine Deneuve when he won the Palme d'Or at the May Cannes film festival for his film *The Taste of the Cherry*. On returning to Iran he was greeted by a furious crowd of protesters. In fact, Kiarostami got his kiss by the skin of his teeth, so to speak: Iranian authorities only allowed the film to enter the competition at the last minute.

• **Mind your language** Idle doodling and, perhaps, not so idle note-making led to unexpected results for Latvian student Einars Lielmanis when he sat his English exam in May at a leading Riga high school. Having been set an essay on Latvia's proposed entry into the European Union, Lielmanis wrote critically of government policy. He also wrote, in a space provided for notes, 'Fuck the Russians.' The reaction of his national examiners, many of whom are Russian, was swift and hysterical. The Ministry of Education called a meeting and Lielmanis was threatened with disqualification from graduation. In mid-June his fate was decided: a good grade but no certificate. Use of obscenities and, suggest the Latvian press, the sentiments Lielmanis expressed in his essay, prohibit this.

• **Oh Jerusalem again** The Irish singer Sinead O'Connor and the New Testament have fallen foul of Jewish fundamentalists. The singer withdrew from a concert for peace in Jerusalem after anonymous messages threatening her life were delivered at the Irish and British embassies. The New Testament is threatened by a bill now going through the Knesset that would ban 'the possession, printing, distribution and import of any literature aiming to persuade people to change their religion'. While the bill is directed at evangelical sects from the USA, such as Jehovah's Witnesses who are militant in their pursuit of converts, it was the Vatican which pointed out that the bill could lead to a ban on possession of the New Testament even by members of older and more venerable Christian churches.

• **Sex in Swaziland** Chief Jameson Ndznatabantfu Maseko of Swaziland has banned the use of condoms among his subjects, citing biblical law and claiming that they 'misuse and waste a man's reproductive fluid'.

• **Congo fashion** The new Democratic Republic of Congo has banned leggings and mini-skirts along with any other garments that 'display the female figure'. Young women on the streets of the capital, Kinshasa, have been stripped and beaten by soldiers for being 'indecently' dressed.

• **What goes on** The impact on the publishing industry of judgements against authors is often imperceptible to the public, lost in the murky and deniable world of self-censorship. Publishers can take the decision to suppress works deemed sensitive or dangerous much as censors do, and potential readers remain none the wiser. One such instance recently came to light when not one but two religious edicts effected what a British publisher felt it was safe to print.

First published in 1959 and swiftly branded 'heretical' by Egypt's Islamic University, Al-Azhar, Naguib Mahfouz's *Awlad Haratina* (Gablawi's Children) has been the source of continual agitation against the author. It was *Awlad* that led to the *fatwa* excommunicating Mahfouz in 1989 issued by Sheikh Omar Abdul Rahman, spiritual leader of the militant Gamaat Islamia sect. At the time Rahman was quoted as saying: 'If we had punished Naguib Mahfouz when he wrote *Awlad Haratina*, Salman Rushdie would never have dared to write that book.' This sentiment led in turn to the assassination attempt on Mahfouz in 1994.

Awlad has now been retranslated for US publication by Peter Theroux. Transworld, the British arm of the US publishers Doubleday, has declined to publish Theroux's version. A spokesperson for the company admitted that concerns about possible fundamentalist reprisals were 'one consideration' but took refuge in the more usual and unassailable rationale of 'commercial interests'.

Awlad is currently out of print in Britain and continues to be unavailable, in Arabic or English, in Egypt. The American University in Cairo, Mahfouz's English-language publisher in the Middle East, is similarly disinclined to republish. *SAS*

• **Polish plots** Doubleday has also crossed swords this month with its Polish partners, Amber Publishing, over the Polish-language version of its hard-hitting best seller *His Holiness* by Watergate journalist Carl Bernstein and Marco Politi. Doubleday claims that the newly released Polish version of the papal biography has been doctored to avoid giving offence to Roman Catholics in Poland as well as to the Polish Pope.

Doubleday's representative in Poland, Maria Straz-Kanska, compared the cuts to old-style Communist censorship, adding that the removal of controversial references to Polish history — particularly passages referring to Auschwitz concentration camp — did a disservice to readers. 'Polish history as it was taught in schools after World War II was one big lie,' she said. 'There is a lot to be explained, to be discussed openly.' *JV-H*

• **The media is now a weapon**
Technician Pich Em was killed and two others seriously wounded when seven heavily armed, masked men

opened fire on the local studios of the state-run Television Kampuchea (TVK), in the southern port of Sihanoukville, on the evening of 4 May. He is the third media worker to die in an apparently politically motivated attack in five weeks.

Taking place against a background of intense feuding between the two main parties of Cambodia's coalition government (FUNCINPEC and the Cambodian People's Party, CPP), the paramilitary-style operation was quickly linked to the country's political problems. Pin Samkhon, president of the Khmer Journalists Association, reported that 'The media is now a weapon...in political conflicts,' while Ieng Mouly, minister of information, has warned that 'government-controlled media should prepare to face further political intimidation.'

Clearest evidence for this pessimism comes in reports of FUNCINPEC activity in the area in the weeks before the attack. On 22 April, a senior policeman affiliated to the royalist party, visited the Sihanoukville Information Service with a request that a FUNCINPEC video be broadcast on television. This was turned down on grounds of political content (national television is meant to be politically neutral in Cambodia) as the video featured FUNCINPEC Prime Minister Prince Ranariddh openly criticising his co-Prime Minister Hun Sen and the CPP. FUNCINPEC is also believed to have approached the

station itself with the video, while armed men visited the home of the station chief with the same request, which was again refused. A guard was later placed on television and radio stations in the city, but removed at the end of April.

Although the identity of the gunmen is unknown, observers in the capital, Phnom Penh, have suggested the attack may have been encouraged by FUNCINPEC officials. The party has accused the Information Ministry of utilising the national network to propagate CPP policies and not affording FUNCINPEC the same amount of air time as their rivals. Amnesty International report that officials in at least one other province have received death threats over the past two months in an attempt to intimidate them into broadcasting certain material. Prince Ranariddh himself threatened in March to send tanks to the ministry if its control over TVK was not 'corrected'.

Journalists in Cambodia fear the attack in Sihanoukville, which severely damaged broadcasting equipment and has effectively destroyed the television station, could be the first of many in the run-up to Cambodia's national elections next year. At least five journalists have died in 10 violent incidents in Cambodia over the past three years. *SAS*

• **Egyptian courts stand by female circumcision** On 24 June Islamic scholars welcomed the decision of an Egyptian court reversing a 1996 ban on female circumcision. While the ruling retains the ban on operations performed by untrained practitioners such as midwives and barbers and the use of primitive equipment, it was a serious setback for opponents of the practice.

Although some polls show that between 70 and 90 per cent of Egyptian women have been the subjects of some kind of genital mutilation, the 1995 Demographic and Heath Survey, produced by the Maryland-based Macro International and the Egyptian National Population Council, puts the figure for married women between 15 and 49 as high as 97 per cent.

The practice of female circumcision has been associated with potentially fatal health risks, such as bleeding, infection and complications during anaesthesia, as well as problems in childbirth and sexual relations. Its latest victim in Egypt was an 11-year-old girl who died on 20 June following the procedure.

The health ministry's July 1996 ban on the operation was supported by human rights advocates and by President Hosni Mubarak, but faced strong opposition from Islamic fundamentalists, including many in the medical establishment. They argue the practice is essential if women are to be protected from the consequences of sexual desire. Mohammad Abdulal of the Egyptian Organization for Human Rights has said that it will appeal against the decision.

Sheik Youseff al-Badri, a leading light in the Islamist fraternity and instigator of the campaign against the ban, celebrated the court ruling with his followers. Many Islamic scholars, however, argue that the practice is not justified under Islamic doctrine. Female circumcision, they claim, also occurs widely within Egypt's Coptic Christian minority and may date from the time of the pharaohs.

The ruling highlights once again the strength of the Islamic opposition to government efforts to modernise the health sector and spread public health education in a society still largely wedded to traditional practices and unaware of the dangers. The Islamists have a powerful constituency among the many women who still support female circumcision and will put up a fierce fight should the government appeal this latest judgment. *César Chelela*

• **They shoot donkeys, don't they?** Albania went to the polls on 29 June in a state of full-blown anarchy. The unnatural calm as the vote got under way was held in place only by the high-profile turnout of the 7,000-strong multinational peacekeeping force and the army of 600 monitors under the supervision of the Organisation for Security and Co-operation in Europe (OSCE).

The vote-rigging that gave President Sali Berisha his dubious victory in May 1996 will not be possible this time, claims Franz Vranitsky, head of the OSCE mission in Albania. He does, however, concede that this election is being held in 'unusual circumstances and will not be perfect'. It is unlikely to receive even the lesser designation of 'free but not fair', accorded to Croatia's presidential election earlier in June, but the OSCE will recognise the result whatever it is.

The OSCE's insistence that the vote go ahead has more to do with its own reputation than the state of the nation: it has invested heavily in Albania of both time and money, and there is the botched job in Bosnia to be wiped out. Yet the death toll is mounting — around 1,500 in the last three months and rising at a rate of 100 a week just prior to the elections; there are a million weapons in the hands of a population of three million; and the south of the country is totally beyond government control. Berisha decided against campaigning there after its inhabitants threatened to bring out their heavy-duty armoury — tanks and missiles — if he dared set foot in what is, in effect, an opposition stronghold.

In the eyes of most Albanians the OSCE has little credibility anyway. It was willing to sacrifice democracy and civil rights in the interests of regional stability in 1996, when it endorsed Berisha's election victory: Berisha, it argued to its western members states, was the only hope of controlling not just Albania, but the restless Albanian enclaves beyond its borders in Kosovo (Serbia) and Macedonia. The consequence of that,

argue the cynics, is today's mayhem.

The leaders of both the main parties, Berisha's Democratic Party and Fatos Nano's Socialists, have sworn to respect the results of the ballot. Notwithstanding DP propaganda that a Socialist victory would represent 'a return to Communism', Nano is tipped to win. Berisha has not said he will step down and that, say locals, is the crux of the problem: 'Berisha must go' has been the rallying cry of the majority of Albanians since the collapse of the pyramid saving schemes in March this year. Failing that, they add, the election will simply formalise the de facto split of the country into north and south and institutionalise the state of civil war.

Only one aspect of the OSCE's activities momentarily broke the all-pervading gloom among Albania's chattering classes. In an effort to persuade a population preoccupied with the daily struggle to survive that they could take control of their own lives by exercising their right to vote, the OSCE decided to go in for some election literature on its own account. Their leaflets made liberal use of old Albanian proverbs such as 'The owner knows where his house leaks,' and 'Only the owner can pull his donkey out of the mud.' The response to the latter was that 'given the ready access to guns, the owner was far likelier to shoot the donkey and leave it to sink into the mud — along with the OSCE Euro-donkey.' *JV-H* ❏

HARVEY J KAYE

US notebook

• **Caught in a blizzard** Writing in the Organization of American Historians *Newsletter*, University of Kentucky historian George C Herring accused the Central Intelligence Agency of a 'brilliant public relations snow job'. Referring to the CIA's promise to release records on its covert Cold War operations — the Iranian coup of 1953, the Guatemalan coup of 1954, the anti-Castro Bay of Pigs invasion of 1961 — Herring, a former member of the official CIA Historical Review Panel, called the Agency's proclaimed 'openness' a 'carefully nurtured myth'. Agency officials at first denied Herring's assertions, but added that they had to be careful in releasing old records for fear of endangering people. They then announced that various files on 1950s operations had been destroyed back in the early 1960s, among them those on the Iranian coup. At the same time, they released 1,400 pages of documents on the Guatemalan coup.

On 19 May the Federation of American Scientists filed a lawsuit seeking to compel the CIA to reveal the size of its 'black budget', the funds provided specifically for espionage today.

• **Not while on duty** The US army is revising its anti-drug policies. Soldiers enrolled in the Native American Church will now be allowed to participate in religious rituals involving the consumption of peyote, a cactus with hallucinogenic properties. Civilian Native American Church members were already entitled to use peyote for religious purposes under the American Indian Religious Freedom Act as amended in 1994. However, the military stipulates that peyote must not be brought onto a military base, and consumption must have ceased 24 hours prior to a return to duty.

• **Ralph, Randy and Rupert** Christian Coalition leader Ralph Reed has announced that he will step down as head of the organisation in September. Appointed to the post by the group's founder, televangelist Pat Robertson, Reed turned the Coalition into a powerful force on the Republican right — originally gaining notoriety for his strategy of running 'stealth candidates' for local offices (such candidates were not to declare their fundamentalist faith and Christian politics until after they had been elected).

Reed plans to set up a consulting firm to promote 'pro-family, pro-life, pro-free-enterprise' candidates, though he has not ruled out running for political office. Reed's departure coincides with a Federal Election Commission investigation into whether or not the Christian Coalition violated its tax-exempt status by directly supporting Republican candidates.

The organisation has announced that former Republican Congressman Randy Tate, elected to the House in the Gingrich landslide of 1994 but defeated in 1996, will be taking Reed's place. In Congress Tate avidly supported the Coalition's agenda, not to mention that of the National Rifle Association, including repeal of the federal prohibition on assault weapons.

In the wake of these announcements came the startling news that Pat Robertson had agreed to sell his cable TV Family Channel to Rupert Murdoch's News Corporation. Given the irreverent and sexy fare broadcast on Murdoch's Fox television network, the *New York Times* called the sale a 'merger of the sacred and profane'.

• **Onward Christian soldiers** By no means is the Christian Right giving up the culture wars. The *New Republic* reports that groups like Family Friendly Libraries (FFL) have stepped up their campaigns against the American Library Association (ALA), an organisation the FFL contends promotes a 'pro-gay, anti-family radical agenda'. Seeking to avoid charges of censorship, the FFL does not call directly for a purge of subversive literature, but demands that librarians place tighter limits on children's access to books deemed 'hostile to family values'.

And speaking of books: under pressure from Southern Baptist groups, the International Bible Society has cancelled plans to publish a new gender-neutral edition of their bestseller, *The New International Version of the Bible*, in which 'men' would have become 'people'. ❏

Harvey J Kaye is the Ben & Joyce Rosenberg Professor of Social Change and Development at the University of Wisconsin-Green Bay. His book 'Why Do Ruling Classes Fear History?' And Other Questions *has just been released in paperback by Macmillan*

BRUCE SHAPIRO

Zero-tolerance gospel

Law and order evangelists are out on the streets of New York brutally tidying away crime and indigence. They claim a high rate of success — but theirs is not the only way

A T lunchtime on 20 June, New York City police descended on Washington Square Park, the bustling Greenwich Village oasis at the foot of Fifth Avenue. Seeking to serve warrants on small-scale marijuana dealers who quietly hawk their product at passers-by from park benches, the police sealed off the park's exits, trapping hundreds of law-abiding citizens inside. A Rutgers University professor was detained in handcuffs when he tried to leave to make an appointment. 'There were a lot of mothers with baby carriages and children,' one witness told the *New York Times*. The total haul from 58 people arrested for sale or possession: a mere pound and a half of marijuana.

Welcome to zero-tolerance policing, the strategy New York's Mayor Rudolph Giuliani claims is responsible for a reduction in crime so drastic that the city is now among the safest in the US. After being elected in November 1993, Giuliani appointed a new police commissioner named William Bratton, and declared that no offence was too small — not begging in doorways, single-joint marijuana sales in public parks, squeegee hustles in traffic — and no offender too low-level to escape police attention. More than a strategy, their approach has become a law-enforcement faith, variously known as zero-tolerance policing, broken-windows policing, or quality-of-life policing (depending on whether the speaker wants to appear tough, intellectual or socially concerned). It is emulated by police departments from New Orleans to New Hampshire.

Now the zero-tolerance gospel has gone international: in Britain, Labour Home Secretary Jack Straw is one convert; so is Ireland's incoming prime minister, Fianna Fail party leader Bertie Ahern, who in May took the zero-tolerance pledge at a campaign press conference with Bratton's Irish-born deputy John Timoney at his side.

Yet the zero-tolerance movement has a darker side, hinted at by that mass detention in Washington Square. In New York, civilian complaints of excessive force — police brutality, in other words — have risen 41 per cent since Giuliani put the policy into effect. Three-quarters of those complaints are filed by African-American or Latino citizens, against a police department which remains 75 per cent white. Amnesty International last year reported that court settlements and judgments paid out by New York City to compensate police brutality victims rose from US$13.5 million in 1992 to more than US$24 million last year; Amnesty charges that under Bratton and his successor many cases of police violence in New York violate basic human rights standards. It's the same in other cities that have adopted zero-tolerance policies: in Houston, for instance, black ministers have repeatedly charged police with openly racist neighbourhood sweeps; in Pittsburgh, police violence became so rampant that the US Justice Department's civil rights division filed a lawsuit and voters this year enacted a civilian review board. Even while zero-tolerance policing enjoys the embrace of ever-growing numbers of politicos on both sides of the water, evidence in the US has gradually accumulated that the strategy has unleashed a wave of police misconduct unseen in decades.

The zero-tolerance faith has its founding document, its Sermon on the Mount: a 1982 article in the *Atlantic Monthly* entitled 'The Police and Neighborhood Safety', written by James Q Wilson, a conservative political scientist, and George Kelling, a criminologist who had studied foot patrols in Newark. Wilson and Kelling's central argument was simple, centred on what they called their 'broken windows' hypothesis: if a factory or office window is left broken, passers-by will conclude that no-one cares, no-one is in charge — and will soon shatter the other windows as well. Soon that decay will extend to the surrounding street, which will become menacing and hostile. Say Wilson and Kelling, it is the small, seemingly insignificant signs of disorder — graffiti, loitering by the homeless, subway fare-

Right: New York 1997: Lexington Avenue, Upper East Side — Credit: Sylvia Plachy

jumping by teenagers — which lay the groundwork for more serious street crime and social decay. The graffiti artists and fare-jumpers themselves, getting the message that social norms will not be enforced, become likely candidates for more dangerous lawbreaking; while citizens, feeling threatened by homeless beggars and squeegee-men, withdraw from the civic arena. So police, Wilson and Kelling argued, should go back into the business of aggressive order maintenance.

With its vivid central image and its implied rejection of economic or social explanations of crime, the broken windows hypothesis proved instantly appealing in politics. And it is grounded in a sensible core perception: an environment of physical safety is one important element of any civil society. Few urban dwellers have not raged against the absentee landlord down the block whose crumbling tenement shelters crack dealers in the cellar, have not felt some relief when a police officer quietly intervened with a deranged, intoxicated stranger talking to himself on the stoop while children play nearby. Prior to 'The Police and Neighborhood Safety', few US police departments paid attention to what Jane Jacobs calls the 'small change' of urban life; their crime-fighting strategy consisted of cruising streets in squad cars, waiting for trouble. As Kelling writes with attorney Catherine Coles in his most recent book, *Fixing Broken Windows* (Free Press): 'Most police considered themselves too busy responding to calls for service and dealing with serious crime to give attention to disorder.'

In the 1980s the broken windows hypothesis found its first great test in New York City's subway system. William Bratton, then head of the transit police, decided to take on the fare-jumpers and graffiti artists his officers had previously ignored. The results were notable: robberies dropped, passengers felt safer in a cleaner, more orderly system, and Bratton's transit indeed found some of their minor public-order arrests snaring higher-level offenders. (The most famous such case came last year, when a mentally ill multiple-murderer who was terrorising the affluent Upper East Side was arrested for turnstile-jumping.)

But enforcing a strict public-order philosophy in the confined, fare-paying venue of a subway is one thing; in the open air of city neighbourhoods, quite another, as that Washington Square trawl and New York's police brutality figures suggest. The brutality figures in particular are to a large extent inevitable with the zero-tolerance approach. As studies by the US Justice Department and university researchers have documented, police brutality is most likely to begin with a citizen's casual defiance of an officer on a minor public-order matter — say, a traffic stop, which led to the police shooting of Johnny Gammage in Pittsburgh last year, or intoxication, the condition in which Archie Elliot of Prince George's County, Maryland was shot 14 times in the back while handcuffed in police custody. For many police officers, 'zero tolerance' and 'public order maintenance' are seen as a mandate to assert their authority at any cost. 'Is the level of complaints an appropriate trade-off?,' Bratton recently said in *Newsweek*. 'I think so.'

And this is not just a matter of a few excesses on the street but of deliberate obfuscation by zero-tolerance theorists. In *Fixing Broken Windows*, Kelling and Coles don't even mention police brutality as a policy issue, though they attack civil libertarians for trying to restrict police conduct. In one particularly telling omission, Kelling and Coles elaborately praise a public campaign that took back New York's Grand Central Station from the legion of homeless people who sought shelter there in the 1980s. They offer not even a footnote acknowledging that beatings by a notoriously brutal goon squad — documented on the front page of the *New York Times* — did much of the taking back.

The zero-tolerance crowd also ignore a longer-term consequence of their neighbourhood sweeps and other minor-violation round-ups: the erosion of police legitimacy. Prior to Giuliani's election, New York City police under Commissioner Lee Brown (the man Bratton replaced) worked hard to build trust between police and neighbourhoods throughout the city. Bratton and Giuliani discarded that approach. 'The larger concern about zero tolerance,' warned a recent study commissioned by the decidedly law-and-order US Congress, 'is its long-term effect on people arrested for minor offenses.' The study goes on:

> Even while massive arrest increases, such as those in New York City, may reduce violence in the short run...they may also increase serious crime in the long run. The negative effects of an arrest record on labor market participation are substantial. The effects of an arrest experience over a minor offense may permanently lower police legitimacy, both for the arrested person and their social network of family and friends.

Indeed, in the US zero-tolerance policing is really an extension of a national zero-tolerance policy towards low-level drug users and similar

offenders which has tripled the national prison population since 1985 to
1.6 million, including one-third of all African-American men under 25;
according to a new study from the Sentencing Project of Washington, DC,
the US incarceration rate is now matched only by Russia. This is zero
tolerance with a vengeance. As Nicholas Pastore, former police chief of
New Haven, Connecticut, has observed, the US has an entire generation
growing up 'prison-educated and prison-behaved'. The public
consequences may prove disastrous, since sooner or later all but the most
violent of these offenders reach the end of their sentences and will wind
up back on the streets.

If zero-tolerance evangelists underplay the policy's dangers, they
equally overstate its contributions to the declining crime rate. Their case
is unquestionably aided by the coincidence of Mayor Giuliani's mayoralty
and the declining crime rate in New York City. But few serious scholars
attribute that radical decline principally to the mayor's police reforms.
There's a strong case to be made that some of New York's precipitous drop
in crime is owed to policies enacted by Giuliani's predecessor, Mayor
David Dinkins, who Giuliani, a former federal prosecutor, campaigned
against as a soft-on-crime liberal. It was Mayor Dinkins and his police
commissioner, Lee Brown, who returned crime-prone teenage truants to
school in large numbers, who added 3,000 new officers to the force and
shifted hundreds of others from desks to the street. Other likely factors:
increased employment, with even marginal low-wage jobs siphoning off
young people from the underground economy; a natural levelling of the
crack market, source of so much wild-west violence in the late 1980s and
early 1990s; and regional demographic shifts, with fewer people of the
most crime-prone age out there, period.

Furthermore, there are other schools of police reform which effectively
encompass quality-of-life issues without recourse to the heavy-handed
zero-tolerance approach. In New Haven, one of the nation's most
impoverished and violence-plagued cities, police chief Pastore saw crime
fall just as far after he took the polar opposite approach: he invited
neighbourhoods to work with police in defining enforcement priorities;
made his department a front door for access to social services; put a
domestic-violence advocate in charge of all police training and required
all new officers to spend three months studying child social development;
and recruited officers from city neighbourhoods with the slogan POLICE
OTHERS AS YOU WOULD HAVE OTHERS POLICE YOU. In

Boston, homicide has dropped just as dramatically as in New York: the city had not a single murder by a teenager in 1996 after running over 100 annually in the past — without any zero-tolerance sweeps. Police relied instead on careful computer tracking of the handgun supply line, aggressive follow-up with paroled offenders and carrot-and-stick negotiations with teenage gangs to persuade them to keep their guns at home. The point is that zero tolerance is hardly the only effective police reform to emerge from the US in recent years.

Zero-tolerance policing unquestionably makes for effective campaign rhetoric, and the original Wilson and Kelling broken window hypothesis is an easy sell to any society frightened by seemingly uncontrollable crime. On its deepest level, however, it is not about crime at all, but a vision of social order disintegrating under glassy-eyed liberal neglect. Much of Wilson and Kelling's original argument, and Kelling and Cole's recent book, is devoted not to crime policy but to repeated attacks on civil libertarians, advocates for the homeless and social liberals. Disorder, Kelling and Cole write, 'proliferated with the growth of an ethos of individualism and increasing legislative and judicial support for protecting the fundamental rights of individuals at the expense of community interest'. Over and over, Kelling and Cole blame the 1960s for that ethos: 'the expression of virtually all forms of non-violent deviance came to be considered synonymous with the expression of individual, particularly First Amendment or speech-related, rights.' Civil libertarians even get the blame for the proliferation of the homeless mentally ill in American streets — as if the Reagan administration had not cut their community support programmes and eliminated public housing construction, as if real estate speculators had not gentrified thousands of formerly affordable single-room housing units.

The course of violent crime is complex, and inextricable from the fate of cities and the poor. Here is the real danger of the zero-tolerance gospel: it severs crime from context, and instead of a clear vision of a safe society offers only an illusory obsession with order at all costs. ❏

Bruce Shapiro is a contributing editor at the Nation, *where he writes the 'Law and Order' column. His book* One Violent Crime *will be published next winter in the US by HarperCollins*

ROBIN COOK

Do unto others

New Labour's foreign secretary promises a more ethical foreign policy and puts human rights at the centre of its agenda

We are instant witnesses, in our sitting rooms through the medium of television, to human tragedy in distant lands, and are therefore obliged to accept moral responsibility for our response.

The Labour government does not accept that political values can be left behind when we check in our passports to travel on diplomatic business. Our foreign policy must have an ethical dimension and must support the demands of other peoples for the democratic rights on which we ourselves insist. The Labour government will put human rights at the heart of our foreign policy and will publish an annual report on our work in promoting human rights abroad...

[The mission statement] supplies an ethical content to foreign policy and recognises that the national interest cannot be defined only by narrow realpolitik...

The mission of the Foreign and Commonwealth Office is to promote the national interests of the United Kingdom and to contribute to a strong world community.

We shall pursue that mission to secure for Britain four benefits through our foreign policy:

• *Security* We shall ensure the security of the United Kingdom and the Dependent Territories and peace for our people by promoting international stability, fostering our defence alliances and actively promoting arms control;

• *Prosperity* We shall make maximum use of our overseas posts to promote trade abroad and boost jobs at home;

• *Quality of Life* We shall work with others to protect the world's environment and to counter the menace of drugs, terrorism and crime;

• *Mutual Respect* We shall work through international forums and bilateral relationships to spread the values of human rights, civil liberties and democracy which we demand for ourselves.

To secure these benefits for the United Kingdom we shall conduct a global foreign policy with the following strategic aims:

• to make the United Kingdom a leading player in a Europe of independent nation states;
• to strengthen the Commonwealth and to improve the prosperity of its members and co-operation between its members;
• to use the status of the United Kingdom at the United Nations to secure more effective international action to keep the peace of the world and to combat poverty in the world;
• to foster a people's diplomacy through services to British citizens abroad and by increasing respect and goodwill for Britain among the peoples of the world drawing on the assets of the British Council and the BBC World Service;
• to strengthen our relationships in all regions of the world.

The government will seek to secure these strategic aims over the five years of this Parliament.

In the next 12 months we shall focus on the following immediate priorities:

• the success of the British presidency of the European Union, by opening the doors to enlargement and completing the single market;
• an enlarged NATO and the strengthened security partnerships throughout Europe;
• a successful transition in Hong Kong which promotes its prosperity and preserves its freedoms;
• an agreement on specific measures to protect the world's environment at the forthcoming UN conferences;
• a productive Commonwealth Summit which promotes trade, investment and good government for all its members;
• a deeper dialogue with the countries of Asia through a successful Asia-Europe Summit;
• a vigorous effort to develop our relations with key and emerging partners.

The government will use the professionalism, the expertise and the dedication of the staff of the FCO in Whitehall and abroad to achieve our mission. I invite them to join with us in working together to deliver these benefits for the British people.

Excerpted from the Mission Statement delivered at the Foreign and Commonwealth Office, May 1997

• •

MATTHEW D'ANCONA

Ethics man?

**New Labour's intentions are good but realpolitik and the·
domestic economy may prove greater obstacles than Robin
Cook would have us believe**

IT IS no accident that one of the first things Robin Cook did when he
became foreign secretary was to replace the portrait of Charles James
Fox hanging in his office with a portrait of his Labour predecessor Ernest
Bevin. Like Cook, Bevin (foreign secretary from 1945 to 1951) was a man
of genuine principle: like Cook, he was also a wily pragmatist. The
question for organisations such as *Index*, which monitor human rights
abuses around the world, is which instinct will prevail in the next five
years.

In May, less than a fortnight after Tony Blair's election landslide, Cook
made a robust statement of principle in which he promised to make
Britain a 'force for good in the world' and insisted that political values
could not be 'left behind when we check in our passports to travel on
diplomatic business'. From now on, according to Labour's first foreign
secretary since 1979, this country's foreign policy will have a clearly
identifiable 'ethical dimension'. He has also promised to investigate
Britain's sale of arms to 'regimes that might use them for internal
repression or international aggression'.

We have been here before, of course, and not so very long ago. As
foreign secretary, Douglas Hurd, that archetypal patrician–diplomat,
promised that overseas aid would be explicitly linked to democratic
reform — what he called 'the moral imperative'. How much less
impressive those words seemed when Hurd was dragged through the
courts over the Pergau Dam scandal, in which aid to Malaysia was linked
not to human rights but to trade deals with Britain. Experience suggests

that Cook's grand declarations of principle should be treated with a cellar-full of salt.

In this case, however, experience is not an entirely reliable guide. Whatever one makes of New Labour, one cannot dispute its newness — and one aspect of this is a fierce belief that government is a profoundly ethical business. Anyone who doubts this should consult Blair's article 'Why I am a Christian' in the *Sunday Telegraph* of Easter 1996, perhaps the most candid public profession of faith made by a leading British politician since World War II. His cabinet is the most overtly religious since Harold Wilson's so-called 'Christian family cabinet'. His ministers speak routinely of the ethical imperatives at work in politics.

This is not to say that our new masters are moral paragons. But there is an extraordinary moral garrulousness about them: New Labour is a party obsessed by the interaction of ethics and practical government, gripped by a conviction that the two need not be incompatible. This is why Robin Cook's promises cannot be dismissed as mere politician's cant. Having interviewed the then shadow foreign secretary in March, I believe he means what he says.

Paradoxically, this is the problem. If Blair and his colleagues were willing to 'smile, and smile, and be a villain', then they could mouth as many high-minded platitudes about foreign policy as they wished and then get down to business as usual. But the new government does seem to believe sincerely, some would say naively, that it can escape the constraints of realpolitik and stand for more than national self-interest in its dealings with other countries.

What will this mean in practice? As an aficionado of the Scott Report (see *Index* 2/1996), Cook may well take significant steps to improve transparency in the notoriously secretive arms trade (see *Index* 10/1991). The arms-to-Iraq affair revealed how murky is the world of defence exports, how unaccountable are those who sell and authorise the sale of arms. To make this commercial sector more open — by improving the procedures by which defence exports are licensed and registered — is only a matter of political will.

Beyond this, however, I am not so sure. Blair has promised to be ethical. But he has also promised jobs, growth and prosperity for all. New Labour's plans to reduce unemployment, spend more on education and health, but keep down taxes, depend on its ability to generate growth and create jobs throughout this Parliament. On this, the Blair Project stands or falls.

Herein lies the true dilemma of Robin Cook's ethical vision. After the USA, Britain is the second-largest exporter of arms to the rest of the world: its market share rose from 16 per cent in 1994 to 19 per cent in 1995. The defence trade employs, directly or indirectly, about 400,000 people — 10 per cent of the manufacturing workforce. The Al-Yamamah arms deal with Saudi Arabia alone is worth £2 billion a year.

The truth is that Labour cannot afford to allow the British defence sector to contract. On the contrary: the government needs this sector to expand if it is to make good its promises of jobs and economic bounty. Cook may, as he has already hinted, ban the sale of water cannon to Indonesia as a token gesture. But is he really likely to block that country's order of 16 Harrier trainer jets from British Aerospace — even though similar jets are alleged to have been used against dissidents in East Timor?

And how stringently will the foreign secretary's human rights test be applied to Saudi Arabia, where Blair's religion is banned in public? One has only to look at 'Index Index' in every issue of this magazine to realise how difficult it will be for Cook to resolve this dilemma. Among those nations which are buying arms in the greatest number, 'internal repression' of one kind or another is the norm rather than the exception. How will Labour make good its ethical promises without banning arms sales to all countries in which human rights abuses take place?

'The faith of the armourer,' as George Bernard Shaw wrote, is 'to give arms to all men who offer an honest price for them without respect of person or principles'. This is not New Labour's faith. But it remains to be seen how far Cook's moral vision will become reality, and how long the pressures of realpolitik can be kept at bay. At the very least, the struggle between the man of principle and the pragmatist will be a fascinating one to behold. ❏

Matthew d'Ancona is deputy editor (Comment) of the Sunday Telegraph

CAROLINE MOOREHEAD

Deadly harvest

The new British government gives a boost to worldwide moves to ban landmines

Cambodia 1997: still the killing fields

EARLY in the morning of 18 September 1996, a group of Angolan children set out together for school from their homes in Bairro Muqueneno. There were 12 of them; the youngest was six. They hadn't gone far before one stepped on a landmine, concealed by the edge of the road. It was a fragmentation mine, with an extremely powerful blast. All 12 children died. In Angola's long-running civil war many thousands of civilians died or were maimed by landmines. They go on dying today, for even by conservative estimates, the number of unexploded mines left in Angola ranges from nine million to 15 million. Many of the dead are children: of all the weapons of modern warfare, mines are one of the most lethal to children. Every hour, say the experts, somewhere in the world, three people die or are maimed by a mine.

Worldwide, the figure for unexploded mines, according to the International Committee of the Red Cross (ICRC), now stands at about 130 million, scattered through the fields, along the roads, in the forests, canals and rivers, of 64 countries. Daily life, for those forced to live among them, is terrifying. The numbers grow all the time, as existing stockpiles circulate throughout countries in states of permanent low-intensity war. A landmine, said a Khmer Rouge general not long ago, is the perfect soldiee: 'Courageous, it never sleeps, it never misses.'

The mine that killed Bairro Muqueneno's children was a POMZ, probably supplied by the Soviet Union. The Soviets were identified by an Africa Watch report in 1993 as one of 18 countries sending anti-personnel mines to Angola. With 13 separate types, they were the most prolific suppliers. After them came South Africa, with seven models, Italy and China with three each, West Germany with two.

On 21 May Robin Cook, the UK foreign secretary, and George Robertson, the defence secretary, made an announcement about the Labour government's position on landmines. All anti-personnel mines held by the army, they declared, would be destroyed by 2005 — and possibly sooner. There would also be an immediate ban on their import, export, transfer and manufacture, and their use would be suspended under a moratorium. The same ban, they went on, was to affect the SP233 runway denial bomblet, dropped by the RAF Tornadoes in low-level raids during the Gulf War, as well as 'smart' mines, those that theoretically self-destruct. A programme to develop a new mine is to be cancelled.

Even a proviso, that landmines can be used in 'exceptional circumstances' — if, say, the UK went to war — comes with an undertaking that ministers will tell Parliament if they agree that they may be used.

This announcement, bringing the UK into line with some 30 other nations which have already suspended or banned the use of anti-personnel mines and some 50 which have prohibited exports, was expected by weapons experts — but not so soon, nor with such little opposition from the military. It confirms, says Chris Smith, senior research fellow at the Centre for Defence Studies, Robin Cook's declared desire for an 'ethical foreign policy'.

But what, in the long-running battle to remove what experts see as one of the biggest public health hazards of the late twentieth century, will it accomplish?

The control of landmines has a long, and for the most part depressing, history. The Landmines Protocol of the 1980 Convention on Conventional Weapons, drawn up to lessen the impact of mines on civilians, has proved weak to the point of uselessness, doomed by complicated rules, exceptions, and discretionary language. In 1996, after a two-year review, the Protocol was amended, but the revised document has proved little stronger than its predecessor and military considerations have made themselves heard far louder than humanitarian concerns. Speakers at international conferences have seemed more interested in discussing loopholes and the need for switching to 'smart' mines (which have a failure rate of self-destruction as high as 30 per cent) than in calling for a complete ban. And whatever progress has been made among western countries has been consistently obviated by a total refusal by China or Russia — both major producers and users of landmines — to join in discussions [In June, the Russian foreign minister, Yevgeny Primakov, backed a phased global ban on anti-personnel landmines — ed]. Even President Clinton, who in 1994 was the first world leader to call for the 'eventual elimination' of anti-personnel landmines, has since gone no further than agreeing to stop producing 'dumb' mines, while holding on to existing stockpiles and continuing to produce 'smart' ones, even after 15 distinguished retired US military officers, among them General Norman Schwarzkopf, commander of Desert Storm, declared in an open letter in the *New York Times* not long ago that a total ban would be 'not only humane, but also militarily responsible'.

The ban on chemical weapons in the 1920s came about as a result of revulsion at their use in World War I. Only a similar revulsion, say weapons experts, can bring an end to landmines, a global disgust so total, and possibly even attached to the granting of aid, that they become unacceptable. In all parts of the world, there are now encouraging signs of this happening, suggesting that the world public may achieve what governments have been slow to promote. The International Campaign to Ban Landmines, set up by a number of non-governmental organisations in 1991, now has over 900 members, and is supported by the ICRC, UNICEF and the UNHCR. The Organisation of African Unity has endorsed a total ban and in September 1996 six central American states declared themselves a mine-free zone. Canada, meanwhile, has sponsored a conference in Ottawa in which states agreed to a final declaration calling for a comprehensive ban, and has announced that it will host a conference to sign a ban treaty at the end of 1997. On 10 December 1996 the UN General Assembly passed a resolution, by 156-0, with 10 abstentions, urging nationals to 'pursue vigorously' a total ban. Even the Taliban in Afghanistan are lending unexpected support, having recently pronounced landmines to be 'un-Islamic'.

The signs for a ban, then, if not good, are at least decent, and Robin Cook's pledge that he intends to be properly committed to the Ottawa process is encouraging, particularly if it is backed up by a clear message that Britain considers landmines abhorrent, in whatever form, for whatever use. But what of the 130 million existing landmines, waiting to explode? Landmines can be cleared, and are being cleared — but at a price. The irony is that a weapon that can cost as little as US$3 to make may cost up to US$1,000 to clear. One mine expert can clear no more than 20 to 50 square metres a day. It is highly dangerous work. In 1993 the international community allocated US$70 million for mine clearance. That same year, 2 million extra mines were laid, leaving what has been called a 'de-mining' deficit of some 1.9 million mines for 1993.

After the ban, then, comes a second, perhaps harder test: that of committing money in sufficient quantity to clear mines sown during decades of casual warfare. Britain, whose record on mine clearance, with the Halo Trust and the Mines Advisory Group, is excellent, could lead the way. ❏

Caroline Moorehead is a writer and broadcaster specialising in human rights. She is currently writing a history of the International Committee of the Red Cross

● ●

TERESA HAYTER

New Labour, same language

Rochester prison, Kent, UK 1997: protest against detention of asylum seekers

Approximately 400 asylum seekers are currently detained in British detention centres, held without charge, without trial and without apparent time limit. Over 300 more are held within the prison service. Their detention is arbitrary and explicable only as a deterrent to future refugees. Many go on hunger strike in protest.

Since 1993, 35 detainees have been transferred from Campsfield Immigration Detention Centre in Oxfordshire to prisons, usually on the basis of accusations by Group Four Security, the firm which runs the centre. Removals commonly follow complaints or protests about treatment in detention. In 1996 three Campsfield detainees were sent to Winson Green prison accused of setting fire to a toilet; although the culprit has since been discovered, one of the three is still in prison. Another believes he was transferred after he complained about a pornographic video. There are, again, no charges against these detainees, no time limits for their imprisonment and often no stated reasons for their transferral. And they have little or no recourse to judicial procedure.

On 22 May 1997 a further 15 detainees were removed from Campsfield as punishment for a peaceful rooftop protest in solidarity with an Algerian, AD, who had been inexplicably removed to Winson Green a day earlier. After nearly 18 hours in police custody, they were duly transferred, eight to prisons, including Winson Green and Rochester.

These events took place under the new Labour government. Labour have promised little on detention: a standard letter and policy information sheet merely state that 'delays are at the heart of the problems with the asylum process' and recognise that 'those asylum seekers held in detention can remain incarcerated for unacceptable periods of time'. They did appear to accept, however, that detainees should be held in 'specific detention centres rather than prisons'.

Since the election there has been no discernible change in detention policies or even in the language used to discuss the process. A spokesperson for Home Secretary Jack Straw's office, speaking in response to queries about the recent Campsfield debacle, repeated the litany to which activists have become accustomed: detention is 'used sparingly', 'regularly reviewed' and 'there is no quota' for detentions. The tenor of immigration minister Mike O'Brien's statement, issued on 22 May, was also familiar: 'Wherever possible immigration detainees are held in immigration centres which are secure hostels not prisons. But some immigration detainees have shown, by their disruptive behaviour, that they are unsuitable for detention in such accommodation. In these circumstances there is no alternative to the use of prison service accommodation. … It would be unfair to the other detainees to give great attention to a small group merely because they climbed on to a roof.'

The government says it is undertaking a general review of immigration detention policy. So far, it would seem to be an internal one.

Teresa Hayter is a member of the Campaign to Close Campsfield

● ●

LOUIS BLOM-COOPER

Policing parades

A more distanced, less emotive approach to its concerns would go a long way to enhancing the credibility of human rights lobbyists

THE announcement from the United Nations that Mary Robinson, president of the Irish Republic, is to be the next high commissioner for human rights has been justly received with eager plaudits generally, and with no less enthusiasm from human rights organisations. She will bring to the formidable task of applying the high-minded principles of human rights conventions and declarations a leadership of unquestioned integrity which is much needed. Her background of statesman-like conduct and legal academic distinction should convey a message that has not always been a feature of the pronouncements of human rights lobbyists.

The latest output from Human Rights Watch — *To Serve without Favor: Policing, Human Rights and Accountability in Northern Ireland* is a prolix report (99 pages) of variable quality on such issues as general policing in Northern Ireland, the vexed question of the policing of parades and marches, the policing of the paramilitary organisations and exclusion orders, and the oft-repeated, but unsubstantiated, allegations about the harassment of defence lawyers.

The report's advocacy for dismantling the emergency regime, on the grounds that the anti-terrorist provisions unduly impinge on civil liberties 'and are used by the police to harass and intimidate people', is entirely predictable and unobjectionable, save for its absence of realpolitik. While it is at present politically impossible to banish the emergency legislation at one fell swoop, there are steps that could be taken to remove gradually the more objectionable aspects of the anti-terrorist regime. The closure of Castlereagh Holding Centre, as recommended by every international agency, is one such step that is justly recommended, although the authors of the report might at least see for themselves the conditions before echoing other calls for closure. On the other hand, a recommendation in the report that 'the Royal Ulster Constabulary (RUC) should take immediate effective measures to prevent the physical and psychological ill treatment of detainees,' and that 'officers who carry out such abuses should be disciplined and criminally prosecuted,' flies in the face of the four annual reports (1994-97 inclusive) by the independent commissioner for the holding centres. These contend there has been no physical ill-treatment of detainees during that time within the precincts of the holding centres, and that the code of practice, monitored and supervised by the independent commissioner and his deputy, has proved to be an effective preventive measure. As to 'psychological ill-treatment', there is no knowing whether detainees generally may suffer peculiar stress, but those supposedly engaged in terrorist activities display a high degree of self-discipline and ability to cope with the austere conditions of short-term detention in police custody not entirely incommunicado.

While it is understandable that human rights groups within the Anglo-Saxon legal systems should decry trial by judge alone for terrorist offences (the Diplock courts), and call for the immediate return of trial by jury, it is untrue to say that these courts, operative for over 25 years now, 'have caused a loss of confidence in the justice system'. A more balanced and less emotive approach to a mode of trial suitable for a deeply divided community might be expected from even the most ardent and idealistic members of the human rights movement. And in international legal circles, trial by jury is not a fundamental freedom. Other models of trial are entirely acceptable.

On policing in Northern Ireland the report is not unfair, although lacking in a balanced approach. It rightly points out the deficiency in the complaints system and calls on the Labour government to consider the recommendations made by Maurice Hayes for a police ombudsman. No mention is made of the known fact that on receipt of Dr Hayes's report in January 1997, the then secretary of state, Sir Patrick Mayhew, accepted the recommendations and promised legislative action, which will be forthcoming.

On the acute problem of parades and marches, the report is once again selective, making no mention of the committee under the chairmanship of Peter North (vice-chancellor of Oxford University) into the issue, resulting in the establishment of the Independent Commission of Parades and Marches under the chairmanship of Alaistair Graham, a distinguished public servant from mainland UK, which is at present heavily engaged in conciliation between the organisers of marches and residents. Instead this part of the report concludes, unhelpfuly and tendentiously, that 'Human Rights Watch hopes that the government will take responsibility for its own role, and the role of state policing agencies, in creating the environment within which last summer's [1996] violence occurred.'

The blame for the disturbances which erupted during the marching season in July 1996 is put squarely on the RUC and the Police Authority for Northern Ireland (PANI): 'the marching season of 1996 must be placed in a broader context which recognises and confronts the grievous failure of the police, [and] state agencies involved with responsibility for the oversight of policing...' The report dismisses, all too readily, the chief constable's frustration at being caught in the middle of disputes. It dislikes the wholly tenable view that the events are a reflection of intercommunal conflict and fails to understand the overwhelming effect of unmitigated bigotry that resurfaced last summer.

If the human rights lobby is to achieve optimum results from its insistence on governmental response to the enforcement of human rights, a greater sense of objectivity is called for. Whatever the validity of the cause expressed by lobbyists, a lack of scholarship in their literary output will inevitably detract from the power of the written word. ❑

Sir Louis Blom-Cooper QC, is the independent commissioner for the holding centres in Northern Ireland

OPINION

FRED HALLIDAY

Post-akhundism in Iran

Iran is at a decisive, difficult point in its history. The certainties of the revolutionary period have crumbled, but the shape of the future, and the forces that could determine it, remain obscure

THE IDEA that the present Iranian regime can in the longer run survive, or meet the aspirations of its people, is one that no serious observer can accept. Pressures on it, from without and within, are mounting, and the leadership of the Islamic Republic is manifestly lacking in the will, or policy, to resolve them. There are many possible alternatives; history and the Iranian people will decide which of them shall prevail.

Although much interested in theory, I am not much given to coining new theoretical terms: but in this highly 'posty' age, I offer the term 'post-*akhundism*' as a means of grappling with some of these ideas on the future of Iran: where that great and beautiful country is going, where its long-suffering people may be headed and how the great richness of its culture and land may be deployed for better or worse in the years to come.

The term *akhund* occurs in common Persian usage to denote a clergyman. (It exists in English in the form 'akond', in Edward Lear's poem 'The Akond of Swat'.) Less respectful than *mullah* or *ruhaniun* or *ulema*, it is still a term any believing Muslim could happily use. Post-*akhundism* means, in one sentence, a society and political system in which

Left: Streets of Tehran, 1980s: revolutionary mural — Credit: Kaveh Golestan

this social group ceases to dominate. It is not to be confused, although it certainly will be, with post-Islamism, something that is as remote, and undesirable, as would be the decay or disappearance of any great religion.

Like so many other terms used in political parlance, *akhundism* is part of, indeed a product of, the modern political history of Iran; it came above all to denote the kind of regime and society created by the revolution of 1978-79. The central claim of the regime has been that it is an Islamic Republic, but there are many interpretations of Islam, and many ways of applying its precepts to politics. This is a point which no amount of official rhetoric since 1979 has been able to obliterate, not least within the clergy itself. What Iran has had since 1979 could, more accurately, be characterised not as *jumhuri-i islami* but as *jumhuriyi-akhundi*: not an Islamic Republic but an *akhundi* republic. It is the crisis, and possible demise, of that republic I want to consider here.

One may define *akhundism* by reference to four components. First and most obviously, it denotes the retention, through monopoly or predominance, of political power by the clergy, most evidently in the position of the *velayat-i faqih*, the position of supreme religious jurisconsult or authority, occupied first by Khomeini and then by Khamene'i, but also in the presence of clergy in the top political positions of state — president, cabinet, speaker of parliament, and so on — and throughout the state apparatus, down to local level. Iran, alone of modern revolutions, has not had a ruling party and indeed abolished the Islamic Republican Party (IRP), the candidate to be such a party. But the reason for this apparent anomaly is that, in effect, the network of mosque committees and the clerical apparatus controlling them has functioned as a ruling party: through it, the clergy have ruled. Those in Iran whose slogan now is *marg bar-zid-i velayat-i faqih* ('death to the opponents of *velayat-i faqih*'), have in their own way understood this point very well. It may be that a non-clergyman will become president, or that lay experts, the *muqallidin*, literally 'followers', are brought into the cabinet, but they would be the equivalent of civilian ministers, technocrats or whatever in a military regime or non-party elements in an old Communist regime: in the final instance, and on important matters, they would know who was the boss.

Second, one can understand by *akhundism* the continued and central role of religious bodies, the mosque and the *madrasa*, in political and social life — be this as a source of public and political opinion, an authoritative source of educational and social values, or as a means of controlling the distribution of goods and welfare. Unlike other revolutionary regimes, the Islamic Republic of Iran has not sought to control the economy, leaving this to the private sector, and dismissing economics as, in Khomeini's words, *mal-i khar*, the business of donkeys. But it has taken care to ensure that its base support is minimally provided for.

Third, by *akhundism* one may understand a particular interpretation of Islamic and Iranian tradition, a specific, authoritative, rendering of what is 'true' Islam, 'correct' Islamic practice, 'appropriate' cultural values and the rest. All nationalist and revolutionary movements and states have sought to present, out of the diversity of meanings and currents in their own past, and by importing without acknowledgement ideas from abroad, a particular dogma about what is, and is not, appropriate to their community. The Islamic revolution has been no exception: much that is part of Iranian culture, and of Islamic history, is excluded, in the name of a new, coercively imposed, orthodoxy. This is as true for the whole theory of 'Islamic government', *hokumat-i islami*, and its correlative, *velayat-i faqih*, ideas that would have struck many people in previous epochs as rather odd, if not heretical, as it is for the bans on alcohol and much else in the Iranian tradition that the Khomeini regime has sought to uproot. One of the most unpleasant, and indicative, moments in the history of the *akhundi* regime, and one in which Bani-Sadr played a particularly sinister role, was the cultural revolution, *inqilab-i farhangi*, of 1980. This grotesque event, like that of Mao in China, was designed as much to root out and suppress elements of culture indigenous to the Persian tradition, to impose one bigoted definition of that tradition and of Islam, as it was to confront the supposed source of corruption, the imperialist, western, cultural corruption. Again we see this in the frenzy of those in Iran now so concerned to keep out the cultural influence of the West, to stop consumerism, satellite TV and the rest, the so-called *bombardiman-i tablighati* and the *tahajum-i farhangi*, literally cultural bombardment and cultural aggression, against which militants are now campaigning.

Finally, under *akhundism* we have to include something more unpleasant, more dangerous, more costly than all of these: namely a culture and a politics of coercion, and at times terror, by those in power, such that dissent outside certain limits laid down by the regime is cruelly and remorselessly punished. The Islamic Republic of Iran has not, by the standards of twentieth-century revolutionary regimes, been among the most repressive, or murderous. The pluralism it has allowed within its own camp, and the range of debate it now allows within society, mark it off, to its credit, from the totalitarian experiments of at least two of its neighbours, and from that of most other post-revolutionary regimes. But this relative degree of what one may term conventional repression contrasts with the particular gender-based harassment of women, a petty-minded vindictiveness and intrusiveness of a truly odious kind, that has become its hallmark. Moreover this remains a regime which has committed, and continues to commit, terrible crimes against its own people, to murder, assassinate, torture, imprison, silence, drive into exile, or just plain beat up those it suspects of opposition and of independent thought. Most of those killed by this regime have, moreover, been people who fought for and supported this revolution.

Life under such a regime permits of three options: co-optation, silent opposition from within, exile. Nothing that has happened over the past 17 years, and nothing that is now happening inside Iran, would lead anyone to believe that this form of coercion has significantly, or permanently, altered. There is great discontent within the country, and there is a debate about where the country could, and should, be going. There are those who, occasionally and with great courage, voice their criticisms of the regime, be it in foreign or domestic policy. Some suggest a more or less secular line of advance, others are seeking new solutions and policies within Islam. The fact remains that while some are allowed to speak there are no guarantees, let alone anything remotely corresponding to the rule of law: critics are thrown out of their jobs, magazines are closed, writers are beaten up, others are held in gaol, to rot or die there, and a much larger number are, of course, forced to remain in exile. In one word, this remains a regime that cannot be trusted. Such a lack of trust is the price, the very expression, of *akhundism*.

Post-*akhundism* can, therefore, be defined in contradistinction to this model. In brief, following the four points made already, it would comprise the following: a departure by the clergy from dominant political positions in the country, including the ending of the authority of the *velayat-i faqih*; the restriction of the role of the mosque to the religious functions hitherto occupied by it and the restriction of its influence on law, education, clothing and the like; the opening of a debate on the diversity of cultural and religious options within the country and the recognition that all countries, and not least Iran, exhibit a diversity of religious, ethnic and cultural voices; and the growth of a culture of tolerance, and genuine pluralism, leading to democracy in the full sense of the word. It would not mean that all those responsible for the terrible crimes of the past 17 years were brought to justice: it would, however, require that, as in other former dictatorships, the truth was investigated and known, that the fate of those killed was established and the names of those responsible placed on public record.

Such a process would, of course, involve a broader shift on the very role of religion in the political life of Iran, a shift towards secularism. It would also involve an acceptance that the kind of dogmatic, *akhundi* regime imposed in 1979 was neither wanted by the majority of the Iranian people nor consonant with its traditions and culture nor compatible with its needs at the end of the twentieth century. Far from such a process being 'anti-Islamic' or designed to weaken the religious beliefs of the Iranian people, it would allow Islam of a more free and creative kind to flourish. The Iranian people, in their great majority, have long been and will remain Muslims, but, as in other countries afflicted with fundamentalism, they know the truth of the old saying that there are two kinds of Muslim, those who have Allah in their hearts, and those who go around shouting '*Allahu Akbar*' in the streets. The imposition of the Islamic Republic may indeed, as many wise people have pointed out, itself have contributed to the discrediting of Islam by identifying the religion and its culture with one particular form of regime and society and in so doing have provoked a backlash that sweeps more than the regime away with it.

Much is made by fundamentalists of the dangers of secularism, as if this were equivalent to atheism or anarchy: but no society is entirely secular, and secularism can, therefore, be seen more as a relative separation of religion and public life than as a complete rupture. What form the separation takes, how far it goes, depends on each society. That such a separation is desirable, and indeed a necessary part of modern life, is indisputable.

FEW not blinded by their own dogma can doubt that sooner or later the *akhundi* experiment of the past 17 years will be gone, consigned to the *zabalidan-i tarikh*, the rubbish-bin of history (a favourite phrase of Khomeini's), much as the Pahlavis or the Communist regimes of the post-1917 period were. The signs of this are everywhere: an economy that has declined steadily since the revolution, unemployment, inflation, massive corruption, growing disaffection among the urban population and youth, a foreign policy that has missed almost every opportunity presented to it and which is mortgaged to unrealistic, confrontational goals, a leadership trapped by its own illusions and the need to keep its immediate following in order. In a broader sense the whole project of the Islamic revolution has, in a remarkably short space of time, run out of steam. No-one believes it can produce a better society, in Iran itself or elsewhere. It offers no future. This is not to say that it will fall tomorrow: this is a regime which retains the support of a section of the population; which has built up a set of military and security institutions designed to protect it from challenge; whose leaders, with perhaps 20 years of political life ahead of them, remain determined to stay in power, and who are prepared to imprison and kill to do so. Abroad, the Iranian revolution may be discredited, but the rise of Islamist fundamentalism in a range of countries suggests that for many years to come there will be those who can claim that the great worldwide revolt of the *mostazafin*, Khomeini's term for the oppressed, is continuing.

In a rough comparison one can say that the Islamic Republic is today where Soviet Communism was in the 1960s or early 1970s — heading for collapse, bereft of inspiration or original ideas, but in the absence of an unexpected cataclysm from within or without, able to last for a considerable time yet. Indeed, like Communism in the 1970s, it may show the greatest activity internationally at the moment when it is burning out at home. Where, then, does this leave post-*akhundism*?

While there is little point in speculating on how or when the Islamic Republic may fall, it may be valuable to pose the question of where alternative ideas and influences that could shape the future of Iran and draw on the energies of its peoples will come from. In broad terms, one can identify three such sources: first, political and social currents within Iran, including in this the exiled communities; second, international pressures; third, Iranian history and traditions.

As far as the regime is concerned there is no alternative within Iran other than those offered by its controlled political process. Such alternatives are not negligible, as the 1996 parliamentary elections showed: between the conservatives, the radicals and the Islamic modernisers there are important differences, which might become greater in the future or at a time of crisis. They are, however, all limited both by the need to play the game of the Islamic Republic and by the political and cultural constraints imposed by the revolutionary consensus: few can believe that any offer an answer to Iran's problems, or are even willing honestly to confront them. The majority of Iran's population remain outside this licensed political game and, most important, the majority of them are young. We can only guess at what they think, or know, but on one thing we can be reasonably sure: they are not fooled by the rhetoric of their leaders [as their overwhelming rejection of the 'official' candidate in the May 1997 presidential election demonstrated — ed]. They almost certainly do not want a return of the monarchy, they may remain suspicious of the West, they do not want to see Islamic values insulted, but they may well want economic development, greater access to consumer goods, freedom of expression and of movement. They probably also want peace. They are the people on whom the future of the Iranian political system rests.

In between the regime and the population lies another source, that of the underground or semi-legal political groups. Many of these remain in one way or another active and each offers itself as the alternative to the regime. All have the right to put their views before the Iranian people and have them tested in a democratic way. The refusal of the regime even to allow the Freedom Movement of Iran (FMI) of the late Mehdi Bazargan to operate freely and contest elections shows just how fearful it remains of the opposition. And beyond the FMI lie many others — monarchists, liberals, left-wing groups, Islamic groups and the Mujahidin. Perhaps some of these will play a role in the future, but one cannot assume they will: the fate of other post-dictatorship regimes is that often such groups command less support than they might think.

On the basis of their actions and programmes abroad, the opposition, as a whole, does not impress. Many remain imprisoned by the ideas and quarrels of the past. The monarchists and their ilk dream of rolling the clock back, even if they pretend otherwise. The left has not taken in the consequences of the failure of Soviet Communism and too much of it still thinks and talks in the stilted language of the dogmatic left. The Mujahidin, who have usurped the democratic right of the Iranian people by proclaiming their own president and who subsist on the generosity of Saddam Hussein, the man who has killed more Iranians than anyone since Hulagu in the thirteenth century, have become a sect, heroic in their opposition, suicidal in their political choices, corrupted by a grotesque cult of the personality. Those in the West who have been cajoled into endorsing their claim to be the legitimate representatives of the Iranian people should think again.

The greatest problem with the exiled and underground political groupings is, however, something else: the absence of a coherent, credible, democratic force capable of taking its distance from the regime and its fossilised opponents and offering a modern, open future to the Iranian people at home and abroad. There were those who defended liberal values, whether in the Islamist form of the FMI, or in the secular Mosadeqist form in the National Democratic Front. A particular source of regret — and one that has cost the Iranian people dear — is that both of these currents abandoned their independence, and betrayed the combative liberal legacy they had once defended, by capitulation to other, authoritarian factions. For instance, the initial courageous stand of the National Democratic Front, who were in the forefront of the defence of human rights and the rule of law, ended in tragedy: the great Shokrallah Paknejad, long imprisoned by the Shah, was rearrested and murdered in gaol; Hedayat Matin-Daftari, the surviving leader and grandson of Mosadeq, the man as much as any other who could and should have preserved the integrity of the liberal left, entered into a misguided embrace of the Mujahidin that has, in effect, silenced that tradition.

The issue of liberalism takes us to the heart of this story. Perhaps the greatest crime of the Stalinist left in Iran was to give the term 'liberal' as a term of abuse to the fundamentalists. I remember standing on the streets of central Tehran in the summer of 1979 as the fundamentalist mob demonstrated against the newspaper *Ayandegan* and shouted the slogan '*marg bar liberalizm*', 'death to liberalism'. *Ayandegan*'s crime had been to print the truth and to criticise the regime, not least over the issue of *akhundism* in which all critical or independent ideas are cast as some form of alien conspiracy, and all defence of democracy or the rule of law is cast as hostile to the Iranian people. We hear a lot these days about Iran as a threat to international peace, but on any balance sheet of the past century Iran has had far more wrong done to it than it has done to others — invaded in two wars, its elected government overthrown, its resources long extracted at unjust prices. Yet this should not mean that all alien ideas are to be rejected, any more than it means that all supposedly indigenous ones are to be defended. Iran needs more, not less, liberalism in this sense: that, if anything, is the lesson of the past 17 years.

In any survey of trends internal to Iranian society and politics mention must be made, and is increasingly being made, of alternative conceptions of Islam itself: that is to say, of political and social models that are framed within an Islamic tradition but which are critical of this regime and which may, to a greater or lesser extent, seek to reconcile Islamic ideas and

Iranian reality with what are broadly seen as western or international norms of democracy, development, law or whatever. There is a long tradition in the Middle East and in Iran of what is referred to as modernist Islamic thinking. Such currents were present in the revolutionary period itself, but in recent years a number of names have again begun to emerge inside Iran. There is little doubt that if a gradual transition is to be possible, and if a new political system consonant with discourses and traditions of Iran is to be found, then such thinking has an important role.

However, the experience of other Islamist states, and, by analogy, of Communist states, suggests some grounds for caution about those who, in broad terms, seek to propose reforms from within. The first is that the issue is not one of interpreting tradition, or texts, or culture at all: it is about political power. You are not going to persuade a dictatorial clergyman to give up power by offering new *tafsir* — interpretations of religious texts — any more than you would persuade a dictatorial apparatchik or Politburo member by quoting bits of Lenin or Bukharin. Indeed once the clergyman, or Politburo member, sees a challenge, especially one he cannot dimiss easily as ideologically impure, he will resort to other means of silencing you, of which we have seen some in Iran quite recently.

The other, more complex, reason for this caution is intellectual: to use regime ideology or theology in an instrumental way — to defend a concept such as democracy or human rights or the equality of men and women with useful quotes from a religious tradition — is perfectly feasible and in some cases necessary. To argue and believe, on the other hand, that all these things are indeed to be found in a religious tradition, and that all the resources for conceiving of a modern politics or social order are to be found within a particular religion, is a delusion, just as it was to think they could be found in the Bible or the Talmud, or in the writings of Marx or Lenin. To get caught up in the system of religious thought is to become a victim of it. Much, therefore, as the new trend in modernist Islamic thinking in Iran is to be welcomed, there are serious reasons for doubting whether it can provide the intellectual, let alone political, basis for a challenge to the *akhundi* system. It also leaves out of the question something which only history itself can answer: namely, do the Iranian people want another version of Islamic politics?

THE fate of Communism suggests that the second dimension of influence, that of the international and external, will also play a significant role in the future of Iranian politics, however much the regime seeks to insulate Iran from it. In one sense the whole project of shutting out the outside world is a hopeless one, as other revolutionary regimes — the USSR, China, Cuba — have found. The very ferocity of the current concern with cultural influence from abroad reflects the realisation that this cannot be kept out. Moreover, the pressures of the international system mean that the more Iran, partly for domestic reasons, seeks to play up its confrontation with the West, especially the USA, the more the external will have its impact, through undermining economic confidence, trade embargoes, blocks on credit and so on. There is no way out of this and no amount of circumvention of such pressure — developing ties with China or the Arab world, seeking to play the Europeans off against the USA — is going to make things much better. What this means for the Islamic Republic is that, as with other revolutionary regimes, it will over time be worn down by the pressure of the international system, whether that pressure comes through direct state-initiated policies, such as the USA's 'dual containment' or through more diffuse pressures of the international market or the globalised culture of consumerism, pop music and the rest. The title of an article published some years ago by a British journalist sums it up: 'Nintendo versus the Mullahs'. In the end we may suspect Nintendo will put up a good fight.

Throughout history, and not least Iranian history, societies have been influenced by transnational flows — of people, ideas, culture, goods, ideologies. The irony is that the Islamic regime that spends so much time denouncing external ideas has itself benefited from many of these. The question that is posed for Iran today is whether a similar, creative borrowing can occur, not least with regard to the two forms of external model most relevant to Iran, economic development and political democracy. These ideas are not, whatever chauvinists or relativists may say, peculiar to the West but are aspirations shared, in the modern world, by all peoples and ones to which the Iranian people are as entitled as anyone else.

Whether such a change is possible in the Iranian case, and how far it accords with the sensibilities and aspirations of the Iranian people, depends, however, on the third form of influence mentioned above, namely Iranian history and traditions. I say 'traditions' in the plural because the greatest distortion, perpetrated by Pahlavi monarchs and

Imams alike has been to argue that there is only one tradition in Iran. An essential part of the move to post-*akhundism* lies in breaking the hold the regime now has on the definition of the Iranian past. The Islamic Republic presents by no means the only, and almost certainly not the wisest, model of political leadership and administration in Iran, not only because of its economic failures and its violations of human rights, but also because it denies the very ethnic and regional diversity of a country in which the Persians are at best half the population. The use of a chauvinist, centralist, Islam to crush the aspirations of Kurds and others is one of the most singular disasters of this regime.

One can expect too that the traditions of a vibrant critical press and of public discussion associated with it will also be recovered. In a broader cultural perspective the hedonistic, doubting, wine-loving *qhazal* of Hafiz and Sa'adi will have as much place as the sermons of the mullahs from Qom; the philosophy of al-Ghazali will be as central as the dogma of the ayatollahs; the music, literature, humour and alcohol of the Iranian people will be recognised as just as much theirs as the one-dimensional definitions of the cultural revolution. Not least, the Iranian people will be able to recapture perhaps their greatest cultural inheritance, their mordant sense of humour: the first person to edit and publish the Joke Book of the Islamic Republic, *kitab-i shukhi-yi iumhuri-i islami*, will surely have produced a bestseller, and a repository of much popular, traditional wisdom. The future of Iran involves a reappropriation of the past — above all it involves taking the definition of that past away from those who have done it so much violence with their simplistic, and in many cases ignorant, codifications. ❏

Fred Halliday *is professor of international relations at the London School of Economics & Political Science. His* Iran: Dictatorship and Development *was published by Penguin in 1978. His most recent book is* Islam and the Myth of Confrontation *(I B Tauris, 1996). Five of his books have been translated into Persian*

Edited from a paper presented at the Centre for Iranian Research and Analysis Conference, UK

INTERVIEW

JOHN JENNINGS

Dangerous liaisons

SHELL PHOTO SERVICES

John Jennings

*A*ccording to Brian Anderson, the UK head of Shell's operations in Nigeria, everything in that country is back to front. 'The government is in the oil industry and the oil industry is in government.' An incident earlier this year illustrates his point well. Over 100 Shell workers were taken hostage by villagers in Warri to protest against the relocation of a local government office. This situation *is by no means confined to Nigeria or to Shell. As corporations become entrenched in the political and economic structure of the areas in which they operate, they are forced to confront this reality.*

In November 1995 Ken Saro-Wiwa and eight other Ogoni activists were executed by the Nigerian government after being convicted of inciting the murder of four Ogoni leaders. The executions caused an international outcry and Shell's activities in Nigeria were thrust into the unwelcome — and unaccustomed — glare of international scrutiny. Accusations of everything from silent complicity in human rights violations to propping up the brutal military regime have been levelled against the company. While Shell and the government enjoy a mutually beneficial relationship — Shell clears a profit in excess of US$220 million a year and oil revenues provide 90 per cent of the government's income — most Nigerians (especially those in the oil producing areas) fail to see the positive benefits of oil exploration and production.

In March this year Shell became the first multinational publicly to support human rights in its statement of business principles. Its chairman at the time, John Jennings, discusses the company's role in Nigeria. **Nevine Mabro**

Nevine Mabro *The argument that trade opens up countries in ways that human rights groups and the media cannot do is persuasive. Can you point to ways in which this is achieved?*

John Jennings Trade and investment is at the heart of economic development and the benefits that it brings are self-evident throughout the world. In a country blessed with certain natural resources, the process brings the technical expertise needed to locate and develop those resources and, in the process, brings that technology to the people of the country. In Nigeria, for example, we have about 5,000 core professional operational staff; all but just under 300 are Nigerian. So most of our people in Nigeria are Nigerian. One hesitates to pat oneself on the back, but we do set a certain standard.

As a commercial company, Shell has different priorities and responsibilities from governments. However, if a government of a country is abusing human rights, should Shell abandon its policy of political non-interference?

Our political non-interference is absolutely clear. We do not engage in party politics or make subscriptions to any political party. In the wider sense of energy policy, if we are asked to offer views on, let's say, changes to a fiscal policy which would stimulate exploration, then we respond, and we make no apology for that. We don't see it as an opportunity to put a partisan point of view across. But on the question of human rights our record is there to see. In South Africa, and of course in Nigeria in the last couple of years, we made it very clear that particular matters of human rights are not in accordance with the sort of human behaviour which we would admire.

Can you visualise a situation in a country that might prevent Shell from operating in it, or do you always try to work within the existing situation?

We try to work within it. The drive is commercial, the role is commercial and what we do is commercial. One way in which a government can make us withdraw is to change the rules of the game such that it is no longer commercial to be there. That hardly ever happens, but there is a perpetual tension — a natural tension — between the benefit to the investor and the government take. However, we try, within the context and framework of acceptable terms and conditions, to be a good citizen; and being a good citizen involves not only obeying the law, but can, on occasion, call for us to stand up and be counted. And we have done so.

Multinationals are increasingly seen as quasi-states. Do you think that in the future they could be subject to human rights and environmental legislation like the nation-state is today? Who would be responsible for formulating and enforcing such legislation?

In the case of environmental legislation, we are already very much subject to a range of regulations. As to human rights — you go into a country and obey the law. If you could imagine — and perhaps this is more theoretical than real — a situation where the human rights behaviour of a particular place becomes so abusive of the basic human rights we all feel we have a right to enjoy, you would have a situation which would be impossible to go into. But things rarely go that far.

Obeying the law in the West and obeying the law in Nigeria, where there happens to be a military dictatorship, have very different implications. Can you foresee a time when there might be an internationally agreed code of conduct to which you would have to conform regardless of the country in which you were operating?

The UN has tried over the years to establish a comprehensive code, but has found it extremely difficult to get sufficient support for any proposal. I think it unlikely that it will find an all-embracing code of conduct. What I would like to see is other multinational enterprises standing up in the way Shell has done. Many others are reluctant. But that is for them to decide.

Despite the fact that the Nigerian government controls 55 per cent of oil exploration and production in Nigeria, Shell has been at the receiving end of the criticism. Why do you think that this is the case?

Clearly Ken Saro-Wiwa was fighting an internal political battle through Shell. Shell happened to be the company in Ogoniland and is a large, successful multinational. He was doing it to bring the issue into the international domain. This was particularly so when it came to the government's failure to live up to its promise of channelling part of the oil revenues back into the communities where the oil was actually produced. The problem was particularly acute in Ogoniland, where the community was not receiving the revenue — three per cent — promised by the government from the limited oil production of about 30,000 barrels a day. Shell has been trying to find ways of ensuring that the government lives up to its promise but it's proving very difficult.

Since the oil industry is so crucial to the Nigerian economy (and Shell is the biggest foreign company in the oil consortium) can you really claim, as Brian Anderson, managing director of Shell Nigeria, recently did, that it has very little influence with the Nigerian government?

The Nigerian government is an independent-minded group. The policies and statements of Minister Etete, its oil and gas minister, demonstrate the limits of Shell's — or any other company's — influence over their policies. They are determined to get the best possible deal they can for Nigeria out of the foreign investor. We give our opinion on questions of energy policy, but the Nigerian government clearly has a mind of its own and makes its own decisions.

Do you feel insecure as an oil company, in the sense that if you don't comply with the Nigerian government, they could replace you, or that your position would be weakened?

The answer to your general proposition is yes, of course they could. Nigeria is a very interesting place from an oil and gas point of view. But bear in mind what I said earlier: we have 5,000 core Nigerian staff and a responsibility to them. In terms of physical security, things have got a lot better in Lagos since the new head of security has been appointed. Things were getting anarchic; in Lagos at least things are under control. There is an assumption that we must have influence, because we produce half of Nigeria's oil. It's an assumption made by someone who doesn't understand the way the oil industry works. We produce enormous amounts of oil and gas here in the UK and we have a voice in the policy debate. It's a healthy system. We can offer our view, but it is up to a government whether or not to accept it.

What do you feel about the view that sees Shell as an independent political body which should be a guardian of human rights when it enters a country?

Put yourself in the position of a government of a sovereign nation: if we started telling them what to do we wouldn't get very far. It's preposterous. So, we are put in our places, as mere members of trade, so to speak, and Nigeria does whatever it wants. But actually, I think we're respected in Nigeria. I went to a hospital in the Delta a week ago, a smashing little place and a joint venture between ourselves and the government. You can't crow about things like that, but I think there are 19 such places throughout the Delta. In a situation like Nigeria, the local communities rely on the oil companies to help replace and provide some of the infrastructural support that the government doesn't provide. We have long accepted that responsibility and last year we spent US$36 million doing just that.

Shell has been accused of enforcing much lower environmental standards in Nigeria than it does in the West. As a result, the livelihood of local communities in the Niger Delta has been destroyed. How do you respond to the allegation?

That is a mixture of several different things. The population of the Delta has grown since we first started producing oil. And, there are many structural problems in Nigeria. How do you actually create sufficient economic growth to allow those people to increase their GDP per capita to the point where they stop having more children or slow down? It's very, very difficult. The oil and gas operations in the Delta have been positive in providing employment and in financing many community development projects in the area. What would of become of those communities without it? They would have remained simple subsistence and agricultural fishing communities. But now, some of them have grown to quite thriving centres — like Port Harcourt; when we were first there it was a tiny little place. It is all part of the process of economic development.

Reports claim that the pipelines in the Delta are above ground and cause pollution and other problems for the local community. Is this true?

Yes, a lot of the flow lines are laid on the surface which was the practice some years back — as in many other areas of the world. The practice nowadays is to bury and cover the pipes. This is in progress in Nigeria now and has been for some years. The whole process should be finished by the end of next year. There is also an ancient sport amongst the people of the Niger Delta: they take a hacksaw and cut a hole in the pipelines. This spills oil onto their fields which enables them to get compensation — which is much more than they would get cultivating their fields. In one part of the Delta they are very good at it and even drill holes. They have all the equipment now.

It has been argued that the West's relationship with the developing world has been defined by its quest for oil. Do you think this will continue to be the case in the foreseeable future?

To the extent that the geology of the earth is conducive to governments controlling it, then I suppose it will. Oil and gas will continue to be in demand certainly for the next 50 years — well beyond, in my view — and countries with the right geology will attract exploration and production of hydrocarbons. And I'm sure those countries will want to encourage it. ❏

John Jennings was chairman of Shell Transport and Trading Company, Shell Centre, London, until 30 June. He was interviewed by Nevine Mabro shortly before his retirement

Great Game in the Caucasus

Since gaining their independence, the countries of the southern Caucasus have gone through civil war, ethnic separatism, coups, assassinations and massive displacement of their populations. Economies and societies are shattered. Meanwhile, the world's powers have gathered to play the Great Oil Game, regardless of the consequences for the people of the region

The research and publication of this feature was made possible by a grant from the Netherlands Ministry of Foreign Affairs in co-operation with the Glasnost Defence Foundation, Moscow

Left: Power play in Karabakh — Credit: J C Tordai/Panos Pictures

IRENA MARYNIAK

Caucasian circles

BEYOND the eastern foothills of the Caucasian mountain range, the road into Baku led across a plain splashed with stains of inky sludge and dotted with disused oil derricks. It was a monochrome sort of landscape with hints of dusty green from broken lines of conifers and odd patches of grass. The sparse buildings were cubes of varying proportions, mostly a dull greyish-yellow.

A little later, we found ourselves in a cramped quarter of the city encircled by Soviet-style boulevards, swerving around potholes on a narrow track between rows of single-storey stone houses with holes for windows and gaps for doorways, opening into tiny courtyards piled high with bric-a-brac. And people walking purposefully in western-style clothing. Further on, past extravagant *fin de siècle* mansions and peaked Islamic arches were pastel green modern blocks overlooking the sea-front. Roughly a third of the flats had satellite dishes poised precariously on balconies alongside lines of washing hung out to dry. Displayed on street stalls, in hotel windows, bookshops, and over the doors of government buildings were images of a thick-faced, heavy-jowled gentleman with a tight-lipped smile. And finally we came to the sea, with those derricks rising once again, like monstrous quadrupeds, out of the water and along the coast line.

Azerbaijan is the oldest oil and gas producing region in the world, with exports said to go back 2,500 years. The first oil wells in the Apsheron peninsula were dug by hand in the shape of upturned pyramids with storage pits beside them. Much of the oil was washed out to sea. At the beginning of this century, following three decades of boom, the oil extracted here accounted for half of the world's production. Huge areas were polluted by bubbling black goo overflowing from wells. The Soviet regime brought new technologies, drilling methods and further ecological devastation. Today, the Apsheron has miles of oil-drenched areas and contaminated subterranean waters with radioactivity over 100 times the accepted level. Azerbaijan's subterranean drinking-water sources are virtually useless.

The first offshore oilfield was constructed here in 1949. It was called Oil Stones and now lies, in an archipelago of floating film and phenols, about 110 kilometres from Baku. Like the Azeri national emblem (an oil derrick surrounded by cotton flowers) this city on stilts remains a symbol of lost and still coveted economic power. Just 70 of the 210 kilometres of platforms built by Soviet engineers are operational. Others are too dangerous or have already collapsed. The hulls of disused wells are rusting and the narrow concrete road which leads around the platforms is studded with yawning gaps, while waves play beneath. The Caspian's fierce and frequent storms send water flooding over the platforms. Between 1984 and 1994, 95 emergencies were recorded on the underwater pipeline at Oil Stones, and on the 28 May platform that spewed out 3,500 tonnes of oil into the sea.

The Caspian is a unique body of water, deep inland, just a little bigger than the Baltic Sea — but with four times as much salt water angrily and unpredictably overflowing its basin. It is rising at a rate of 15-25 centimetres a year (2.5 metres over the past 15 years), constantly threatening offshore and coastal oil fields.

These are the waters everybody wants. They lie at the very heart of a potential system of arterial routes and pipelines between Europe, the Persian Gulf and the Far East. For Azerbaijan, the exploitation of Caspian oil could lead to its re-emergence as a major regional power. The war over the Armenian enclave Nagorno-Karabakh, which declared independence in 1991, heavily depleted Azeri resources and 20 per cent of its territory is still under occupation: Armenian troops control six regions in the west of the country, as well as Nagorno-Karabakh itself. In addition, Nakhichevan, the Azeri enclave bordering on southern Armenia, Iran and Turkey is blockaded.

Azerbaijan is desperate for foreign investment to modernise its ailing industry. Oil profits could help it build an army powerful enough definitively to resolve the Karabakh issue in its favour. It could also potentially reshape the geopolitical map of the region. In Russia, the southern Caucasus is traditionally viewed as an important bulwark against Turkey, Iran and the greater Islamic world beyond. A strong Shia Muslim Azerbaijan, territorially contiguous with Turkey and Iran through its links with Nakhichevan, might conceivably lead to the formation of an

EDGE OF EMPIRE

Dan Smith *The State of War and Peace Atlas* 3rd edition Copyright © Myriad Editions Limited

The break up of the Soviet Union ignited several conflicts in the Caucasus. Russia imposed a fragile peace in some areas even while its forces were bombarding towns and villages in Chechnya.

The Caucasus is home to 28 ethnic groups numbering 5,000 people or more. They differ from each other by combinations of language, religion, history, homeland and culture. Mongol, Persian, Ottoman and Russian empires fought over their lands for centuries. Much of the history is bitter. The Ottoman empire killed or starved to death one and a half million Armenians between 1895 and 1920. In February 1944, Soviet security forces rounded up the entire Chechen nation of 400,000, the whole Ingush nation of almost 100,000, and 100,000 others from the north Caucasus, and deported them to Central Asia. They were not allowed to return until 1957.

At the end of the 1980s, greater openness in the USSR encouraged democrats to demand national independence. Their momentum became irresistible and the USSR broke up in 1991. In the ethnic patchwork of the Caucasus, the independence of one ethnic group was to threaten another with subjugation. The impulse towards independence and national rights slipped easily into aggressive chauvinism. Democracy was fragile, economic decline was sharp and political order collapsed. In Georgia, power belonged to the warlords as the country was torn by three civil wars. Armenian and Karabakh forces occupied part of Azerbaijan. Within Russia, a faction in Chechnya saw a chance for seizing national independence. North Ossetian militias drove 60,000 Ingush from their homes.

Russia attempted to reassert itself in the region. It imposed ceasefires in Georgia but was unable to resolve conflicts either there, or between Armenia and Azerbaijan. In Chechnya, what was meant to be a swift campaign to crush Chechen independence in late 1994 became a prolonged war.

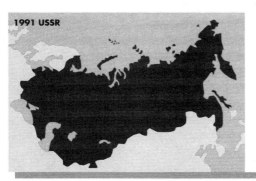

1991 USSR

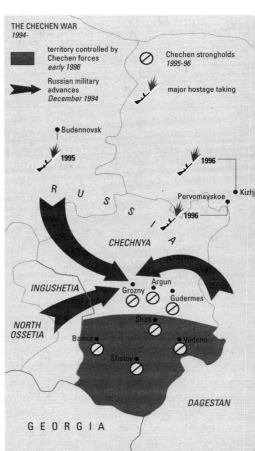

THE CHECHEN WAR
1994-

territory controlled by Chechen forces early 1996

Russian military advances December 1994

Chechen strongholds 1995-96

major hostage taking

Novorossiisk

Gud

Budennovsk

1995

1996

R U S S I A

Pervomayskoe

Kizl

1996

CHECHNYA

INGUSHETIA

Grozny

Argun

Gudermes

NORTH OSSETIA

Bamut

Shali

Vedeno

Shatoy

DAGESTAN

GEORGIA

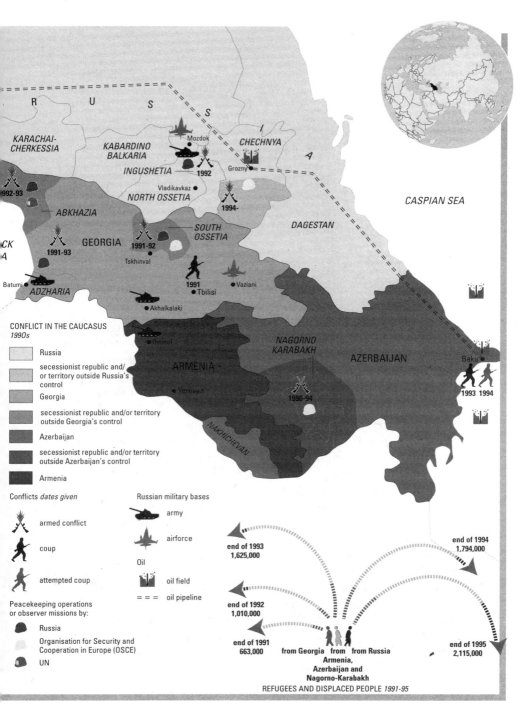

R U S S I A

KARACHAI-
CHERKESSIA

KABARDINO
BALKARIA

INGUSHETIA — 1992

CHECHNYA

Mozdok

Grozny

1992-93

Vladikavkaz ●

NORTH OSSETIA

1994-

CASPIAN SEA

DAGESTAN

ABKHAZIA

GEORGIA

1991-93

SOUTH
OSSETIA

1991-92

Tskhinval

CK
A

Batumi ●

ADZHARIA

1991

Tbilisi

● Vaziani

● Akhalkalaki

Baku

1993 1994

CONFLICT IN THE CAUCASUS
1990s

Russia

secessionist republic and/
or territory outside Russia's
control

Georgia

secessionist republic and/or territory
outside Georgia's control

Azerbaijan

secessionist republic and/or territory
outside Azerbaijan's control

Armenia

NAGORNO
KARABAKH

AZERBAIJAN

ARMENIA

● Yerevan

1990-94

NAKHICHEVAN

Conflicts *dates given*

armed conflict

coup

attempted coup

Peacekeeping operations
or observer missions by:

Russia

Organisation for Security and
Cooperation in Europe (OSCE)

UN

Russian military bases

army

airforce

Oil

oil field

= = = oil pipeline

end of 1993
1,625,000

end of 1994
1,794,000

end of 1992
1,010,000

end of 1991
663,000

from Georgia   from   from Russia
Armenia,
Azerbaijan and
Nagorno-Karabakh

end of 1995
2,115,000

REFUGEES AND DISPLACED PEOPLE *1991-95*

extended Turkic linguistic and religious space which could spread to Central Asia. Those in Moscow who view Turkish policy historically in terms of an attempt to squeeze out Russia from its traditional zone of influence in the Caspian, Central Asia and the Caucasus are understandably anxious.

For the present, though, Azerbaijan has the resources neither to exploit nor transport its oil onto the world market. Indeed none of the Caspian's littoral states yet has the economic, political or military capacity unilaterally to decide on the exploitation of its oil fields. Against the backdrop of latent conflict in Nagorno-Karabakh, Chechnya and Abkhazia, the perennially pending decision on pipelines is crucial. It will determine the choice of markets, the division of profits and the question of who has power over resources. A pipeline means jobs, hefty tariffs and political control. All of which raises the stakes and — in the eyes of potential investors — exacerbates risk (see page 144).

Chechnya and Nagorno-Karabakh have been the sorest points, although the entire Caucasian region is viewed as a potential conflict zone which could stymie effective transport. In October 1995, the Azerbaijan International Operating Company (AIOC) — a consortium of 12 international oil companies — signed deals with Russia and Georgia for two pipeline routes, the northern (through Russia to Novorossiisk) and the western (through Georgia to the Black Sea). Both agreements anticipate the transport of about 5 million tonnes of 'early' oil along each route. The Russian option is cheaper and effectively ready for use but, apart from the Chechen imponderable, there is concern over tensions in Dagestan where Lezgin groupings are calling for their territories in northern Azerbaijan to be returned to Russia. It has even been suggested that Azeri intelligence may be interested in provoking the Lezgins into rebellion at a time when Russia is seeking to establish stability along the pipeline-route — a crucial artery for its survival as a regional power.

A third, and the most natural route for Azeri, Turkish and some western interests, would pass through Armenia, Nakhichevan and Turkey. But because of the dragging confrontation over Nagorno-Karabakh, it is blocked. With recent revelations about arms sales worth US$1 billion by Russia to Armenia in 1993-96, the Karabakh conflict continues to make Russian military and political support a vital or decisive factor in the alignment of forces in the region. If Nagorno-Karabakh were to be formally united with Armenia, Azerbaijan could be politically weakened for decades to come. The country's uncertain internal stability could be threatened, especially in the northern Lezgin or Avar regions, and in the Talysh regions of the southwest, making the exploitation of its natural resources even more problematic. In turn, Armenia's position would be enhanced. With its traditional orientation towards Russia, and the economic and military dependence of Yerevan on Moscow, Russian influence in the region could also be consolidated.

A T THE beginning of the century, Armenia was the country hardest hit by persecution against the Ottoman empire's Christian minority which culminated in the massacres and forced marches of 1915. Today, the one imposing building on the road into Yerevan from the airport is the unfinished — but already grandiose — Russian embassy which overlooks a major intersection. 'The Russians have always saved us,' our driver volunteers, without prompting, 'Armenia wouldn't exist without them.'

Yerevan is overlooked by hilly moorland and — from Turkey — by the great, conical, snow-peaked mountain: Ararat. The city seems half dug-up and tumbling although things aren't as bad as in the early 1990s when the Azeri blockade created an energy crisis which brought Armenian industry to a standstill. Then, with no petrol or gas, horsecarts appeared in the streets and homes were heated with wood-burning stoves contrived from scrap metal. But people still grope their way up unlit stairwells, with gaping holes for windows, into flats where electricity and hot water are cut off almost daily. And in conversation there is a sense of easily ruffled sensibilities and — so often — talk of war.

Journalists — seemingly mild and sensible folk — make chilling predictions of conflict within three months, possibly with direct Turkish, Russian and Iranian involvement. ('This could be a decisive confrontation between Iran and the West.') People speak of daily exchange of fire at the Azeri-Armenian border.

'The Azeris have no clear idea how the oil will be transported,' Avet Demourian, director of Yerevan's Arka news agency, says. 'They don't want it going through Russia; Russia doesn't want it going through Georgia... And the pipeline is just 40 miles north of the front line. A single shot could start something, I think it probably will. If they start sending oil through, it will be a provocation. The interests of bigger powers are at stake.'

The pipeline up through Georgia to the Black Sea still needs to be extended from Tbilisi to a new planned terminal at Supsa. Work is expected to be completed by the end of 1998 — particularly now that the World Bank has allotted US$1.4 million to assess the plan, provide training and technical assistance. In Georgia, the 1995 agreement for transport through Russia is being viewed as an appeasing gesture to a restive power while more serious plans are made for 'major' oil transport along the Georgian route when it is ready.

L YING on the southern foothills of the Caucasus, Georgia has the longest frontier with Russia. In happier times this was the region's land of plenty, celebrated for its feasts and drinking bouts and smiling centenarians. Its capital, Tbilisi, is a crumbling but graceful city, in a broad river-valley surrounded by steep mountainous slopes. There is a sense of concentration here, of claustrophobic intensity enhanced by the chain of hills towering overhead. The seminary where Stalin spent his rebellious formative years is here; as is the home of his henchman, Lavrenty Beria — a palatial neoclassical building with delicate whitewashed columns, shaded by conifers. Like Bluebeard's Castle, its corridors open into dozens of tiny rooms which now shelter Abkhaz refugees. It is in the older part of the town: all higgledy-piggledy clusters of houses rising up the hill, filigree balconies, rubbish tumbling onto the roadway and residues of war. The 'war' here is the stand-off which led to President Zviad Ghamsakhurdia's removal in January 1992 leaving 200 people dead and the city centre in ruins. The old Intourist hotel is still an empty shell; carved facades are pitted with bullet holes and sections of the city centre are still a mass of rubble.

This is another arena in which political and economic battles for the control of the southern Caucasus will be fought. With conflicts in Ossetia and Abkhazia settled into a state of nervous equilibrium, tensions in Adjaria at the Black Sea end of the pipeline route and Russian military bases in all these zones, there is awareness here that an outside hand is on the lever which could determine the country's economic and political future, as well as its territorial integrity. Georgia — economically dwarfed and strategically vulnerable — could find itself caught between the hammer and the anvil. And memories of the dispersal of a peaceful demonstration by Soviet troops armed with toxic gas and sharpened

Right: Aspheron, Azerbaijan — Credit: Russell Sacks

shovels in the early hours of 9 April 1989 are still raw. All but three of the 19 civilians who died were women, and the day has become a symbol of the country's struggle against outside interference. 'All will be well, if only the Russians leave us alone,' Tamila tells me. She lectures in ancient history at Tbilisi University and was brutally clubbed over the head by a soldier who looked barely old enough to be her student.

Exchange visits to Baku and Tbilisi by Georgia's president, Eduard Shevardnadze and Azerbaijan's president, Heydar Aliyev, in February and March 1997, suggest the consolidation of a new Georgian–Azeri alliance within the framework of an increasingly western-oriented diplomacy: a shared desire to be shot of the Russian lever and awareness of the economic possibilities of co-operation over oil under alternative US patronage. A further plan for transporting 'major' oil through Georgia via Ukraine (currently fully reliant on Russia for energy) is also being discussed as part of the new strategic triangle being promoted by Shevardnadze.

And meanwhile, the first batch of 'early' oil is waiting in the Azeri sector of the Baku–Novorossiisk pipeline for transportation by the Russian company Transneft. There have been difficulties with Chechen demands for sovereign involvement in decision-taking and a share of payment along their sector of the route. The security question also remains intractable. But Transneft has preferred to argue in public that technical improvements to the pipeline must still be made, or to seek for loopholes in the transport agreement signed in January 1996, claiming that the oil now trapped at the border was not extracted by the present consortium, but by the state company of Azerbaijan. In response, the AIOC has raised doubts about the viability of the partnership with Transneft: its head, Terry Adams, has threatened an appeal to international arbitration and to demand reimbursement for the US$60 million invested in the reconstruction of the Russian pipeline.

In April, the Georgian media reported that the Chechen government was intending to order a heavy consignment of piping from the Rustavi metallurgical plant in Georgia. As another finger slips into the pie, the vision of a stable route for transport and trade across the Caucasian isthmus is as nebulous as ever. Except perhaps to the boldest, the obstacles to the revival of this stretch of the Great Silk Road, once linking Europe and Asia along the untamed frontier between Christianity and Islam, continue to be awesomely daunting. ❏

RAMIZ ROVSHEN

Recognising

In the darkness birds recognised
each other from their calls.
The cruel angel of death
recognises the swan from the swan song.

I am a different bird, a different bird,
half nightingale, half owl.
Such a big bird I am,
and I recognise the world because of my cage.

... However much I wash my face
I am shocked when I see myself.
When a man dies he recognises
himself in his last breath.

Untitled

I myself flew like a bird
and settled on you as if you were a branch.
I believed in you, my promise,
and I was deceived by you.

I turned my face from the world,
I loved just you and was loved by you.
I tasted only you,
and got used to only you.

You put a spell on me,
we were together as eyebrow and eye.
I lay on you as
a brick lies on the wall.

*Ramiz Rovshen (born 1946) is an Azerbaijani poet, short story and script
writer and an active participant in the human rights movement in Azerbaijan*

VAGIF BAYATLY ONER

Don't look for secrets in this world

Don't look for secrets in this world.
This world seems to have no secrets,
don't look for a place to live.
There is no place even for the dead.

There is no wire to hang yourself on.
There is no-one mad enough to love.
There is no way forward,
and no way back.

Oner became pain itself,
but there is no pain but pain comes back.
I saw God and he was here,
but he did not turn his face to me.

The people who are fed up to the teeth from truth

Today we told each other so many lies,
and now we proudly stand here
because we have told such beautiful lies.
Compared to our lies
the biggest truths of the world are nothing.
Only we could choose
the truths from the lies,
and the lies from the truth.
Because only we know
that the biggest truth is the biggest lie.
Only we who are fed up to the teeth from truth
could shout 'Long live lies!'

Vagif Bayatly Oner (born 1948) is an Azerbaijani poet, born in a region of the country now occupied by Armenia. He is active in the Azerbaijan human rights movement

Poems translated by Richard McKane

ARIF YUNUSOV

Refugee camp, Yerevan, Armenia: exiles from Baku

Demographic disaster

After three years of an inconclusive ceasefire there is still no prospect of peace nor any hope of Azerbaijan's huge refugee population returning home

AZERBAIJAN was the first post-Soviet republic to face a refugee problem. Meetings and demonstrations began in neighbouring

Armenia in autumn 1987 demanding the transfer of the mainly Armenian-populated enclave of Nagorno-Karabakh from Azerbaijani to Armenian jurisdiction. Clashes between Armenians and Azerbaijanis in many areas of Armenia led to the exodus of the first hundreds of Azerbaijanis from Armenia. By the end of January 1988, this figure had reached more than 4,000. This was the first time there had been refugees on Soviet territory since the end of World War II, but the Soviet leadership was quick to ban any mention of the subject, and quickly settled the refugees in and around the Azerbaijani city of Sumgait.

The situation worsened rapidly when full-scale war between Armenia and Azerbaijan broke out in February 1988. By the beginning of 1990, all Azerbaijanis, as well as Muslim Kurds — some 186,000 people — had been forced from Armenia into Azerbaijan. The entry of Soviet forces into Azerbaijan's capital, Baku, in January 1990, and the bloody aftermath, saw a new wave of migration. More than 100,000 Russians, mostly families of soldiers, left Azerbaijan. In turn, 279,000 Armenians had fled Azerbaijan for Armenia; a further 44,000 headed for Russia.

At about the same time, in June 1989, over 50,000 Meskhetian Turks, fleeing potential massacre in Uzbekistan, also sought refuge in Azerbaijan.

The collapse of the Soviet Union, and the resulting independence for Azerbaijan and Armenia in 1991, turned the Karabakh conflict into an international affair. In autumn 1991, with Russian help, the Karabakh-Armenian forces began an offensive and by the following summer had driven the entire local Azerbaijani and Kurdish population from Nagorno-Karabakh and from the Lachin region wedged between Karabakh and the Armenian border. Those driven from their homes, officially known as internally displaced persons (IDPs), swelled the number of refugees. The resulting counter-attack by the Azerbaijani army drove the Armenian population from the Shaumyan region to the north of Karabakh.

By the end of 1993, political chaos in Azerbaijan and the power vacuum in the capital enabled Armenia to occupy six districts of Azerbaijan outside Nagorno-Karabakh. The flood of refugees from these regions became so intense that it jeopardised the social and economic stability of Azerbaijan. Fearing social revolt, the Azerbaijani authorities closed all the roads from the conflict zone to Baku and other major towns in summer 1993. Refugee camps mushroomed along these roads.

The signing of the Karabakh ceasefire agreement in May 1994 allowed the authorities to stabilise the situation in Azerbaijan and to get a grip on the problem of the IDPs. The continuous movement of the IDPs and their simultaneous registration in several locations created some confusion over numbers. In December 1993 the government announced a figure of 780,000 refugees. Together with the earlier refugees from Armenia and Uzbekistan, there were over one million refugees and IDPs on Azeri soil.

However, by 1 January 1997, revised figures put their combined number at 843,000, some 11 per cent of Azerbaijan's population. Independent experts put the figure nearer 750,000.

Regardless of precise numbers, the seven-year conflict has brought about vast changes in the demographic and religious make-up of Azerbaijan. Before the conflict began, Azerbaijan had a population of just over 7 million, of whom 83 per cent were Azerbaijanis; 87 per cent of the population were Muslim, 12.5 per cent Christian and 0.5 per cent Jewish.

The Slav population, mostly Russian, was also heavily affected. Official figures show that after 1989, some 169,000 Russians, 15,000 Ukrainians and 3,000 Belarusians emigrated (the Russians claim that as many as 220,000 Russians departed, leaving around 180,000). Most left between 1990 and 1992, worried by the political instability; for those who left later, the primary motivation was economic.

In all, more than 600,000 non-Azeris left the republic after 1988, most of them Christians: 323,000 of the 390,000 Armenians living in Azerbaijan fled, those that remained were in Armenian-controlled Karabakh. By 1 January 1997, with the total population around 7.5 million, Azeris made up 90 per cent of the population; Christians had fallen to only four per cent of the population. The Muslims' share of the total had risen to 95 per cent.

Behind these dry statistics lie the pain and suffering of huge numbers of the population, regardless of nationality, faith or current location. Refugees are the most vulnerable sector of the population. Over and above the problems afflicting the whole population — the severe economic crisis, the fall in production and unemployment — refugees face their own specific problems. Almost all are victims or witnesses of violence inflicted during military operations or were forced to flee their homes under fear of death. Many have developed psychiatric problems or have needed medical treatment.

The refugees also face serious psychological difficulties in their new places of residence. Most are from small villages and those who settled in towns have taken some time to adapt. There have been cases of conflict with local residents. Today the refugees face new and paradoxical dangers. When the Karabakh ceasefire halted military operations in May 1994 the refugees hoped their lot would soon improve. But negotiations have dragged on and the refugees have had to find ways of surviving, always in competition with the local population. If the talks drag on too long and the economic situation gets worse, there could be serious tensions, above all in the large cities.

Refugees still living in camps face another set of problems. While they do at least receive aid supplies, any hint that aid might be cut off causes an outbreak of panic which could lead to uprisings. The first signs of this were evident at the end of 1996 when a number of aid agencies halted their work in Azerbaijan.

Life in a camp is unnatural and unsettled. Camps are often built without regard for the mentality and previous way of life of the refugees. People of different levels of education, profession and traditions are lumped together. Where the refugees depend totally on outside help, this has led to numerous arguments and conflicts of interest. Life is particularly hard for women and girls, as neither the state agencies nor aid organisations bear in mind their particular needs when building the camps or distributing the aid.

These difficulties have led to severe crises within many refugee families. Men seek fruitlessly for work, many women secretly turn to prostitution as a means of survival and many children cannot go to school as the uniforms and books are too expensive. This environment is also a breeding ground for crime.

Migration did not cease when the fighting came to a stop. On the contrary, the most active refugees, above all the young, migrate to neighbouring countries. Unable to find work in Azerbaijan, they have gone to Russia, Turkey and Iran. In Turkey and Iran they work mainly on building sites, as labourers or as shepherds, earning some US$100–150 per month, plus board and lodging.

But Russia is still the most common destination. The Azerbaijani press reckons that more than 1.5 million left for Russia between 1993 and 1996 and that the number of Azerbaijani citizens now working there is between 2 and 3 million, some 30 per cent of Azerbaijan's total population.

The Russian press has reported that the Azerbaijani community, among which there is an increasing number of refugees, is a significant force in

Azerbaijan 1996: railway-wagon homes for Azeri refugees from Karabakh
— Credit: Jon Spaull/Panos Pictures

business, including criminal business. About one million of this community live in Moscow and the surrounding region. A significant number of refugees in the 20–40 age range, while officially registered in Azerbaijan, find illegal trading jobs lasting several months in Moscow and other major cities across Russia.

The exodus of such a large proportion of the population, even if only temporary, will also cause problems for the nation itself. Most of those leaving Azerbaijan are men, the overwhelming majority of them unmarried. The ratio of the sexes has thus been unbalanced. Given the significant number of those killed, wounded or crippled, many women are doomed to remain single. ❑

ArifYunusov is a historian based in Baku

Translated by Felix Corley

NEZAVISIMAYA GAZETA

A suitable case for destabilisation

B Y THE end of 1994, with the radical changes in Transcaucasia, Russian diplomacy was afflicted with a new headache. On 20 September 1994, the first contract for the Caspian oil super-project, involving the participation of western companies and capital investment totalling some US$7.5 billion, was signed. The project's chief co-ordinator was the Azerbaijan International Operating Company (AIOC), controlled by US and UK capital. This first 'contract of the century' was followed by others in which western oil companies also predominated.

By that time, Russian diplomacy had suffered a threefold defeat: first, it had not managed to strengthen the political forces in Azerbaijan that looked to Russia; second, despite the Russian Foreign Ministry's ongoing efforts to cast doubt on the legal standing of the contracts that had been concluded, citing the uncertainty over the Caspian Sea's legal status, the participation of the Russian oil company LUKoil in these super-projects had the effect of downgrading Russia's official position over the status of the Caspian; third, it had not proved possible to prevent the very real arrival in Azerbaijan of some of the most powerful western companies with large sums of money. Naturally, this could only weaken Russia's role and influence in the region, and was later followed by other, equally dramatic, setbacks for Russia in the area. Russia lost the long-term battle for the oil pipelines.

Backed by money from foreign investors, the oil contract may unite most of the countries in Central Asia and Transcaucasia on an anti-Russian basis. For western geostrategists, the situation goes far beyond the bounds of a straightforward oil deal. For the first time, there is a real possibility of them taking advantage of Russia's weakness to gain an economic foothold in these areas, which are geopolitically very sensitive for Russia; to foster the horizontal consolidation of the states of Central Asia and Transcaucasia around new communications arteries that are geared towards one another, thus depriving Russia of control over commodity flows; to help strengthen the fragile statehood of the former Soviet republics through investment; and to create a powerful economic and military-political alliance as a counterbalance to Russia and, consequently, to squeeze Russia out of Transcaucasia and Central Asia for many decades, possibly for centuries.

Let us consider the weaknesses of Georgia and Azerbaijan as key members of a Tashkent-Baku-Tbilisi-Kiev anti-Russian axis.

Experts will recall that Azerbaijan and Georgia joined the CIS after serious reverses in their development, heavy military defeats and losses of territory. Since then, they have tried to use their ties in the CIS and, above all, to use Russia, to resolve the problems involved in restoring their territorial integrity. Georgia and Azerbaijan have endeavoured to draw up a foreign policy strategy in relation to Russia whereby, on the one hand Russia might be compelled to help them restore their territorial integrity and, on the other, international political institutions and public opinion might be used to offset the influence of Russia and guarantee their independence from Russia. At the same time, both countries used their entry to the CIS to give Russia no cause to take more strenuous action to prevent the consolidation of these states on an anti-Russian basis. While neutralising Russian activity in the region, they did everything possible to encourage the process of internationalising the ethnic conflicts; this led to Russia's role as a mediator being diminished.

Implementation of the Caspian super-projects, which involved foreign capital, helped these countries to ensure more active support from the West in resolving their military-political problems.

[Heydar] Aliyev and [Eduard] Shevardnadze have so far conducted their policy successfully, skilfully outplaying Russian diplomacy which, in the Transcaucasian area over the past few years, and particularly since the start of the Chechen war, has completely lost both the initiative and its sense of purpose. In recent times, the Transcaucasian countries involved have been feeding Moscow with totally false ideas about Russia's interests in the region. Numerous publications raise the question of Russia's final withdrawal from Transcaucasia by the removal of its military bases in Armenia. They claim, moreover, that Russia can establish good relations with Georgia and Azerbaijan on a long-term basis only by stepping up the

• •

Operation pipeline

According to a 'well-informed' Armenian source, Russian forces have been exploring ways of putting pressure on the Azerbaijan International Operating Company (AIOC), or taking over the pipeline on Azeri territory, if the oil consortium opts for the Georgia-Turkey route for the transport of 'major' oil to Europe.

The existing pipeline in central Azerbaijan goes past the town of Evlakh, a few kilometres away from territory occupied by the Nagorno-Karabakh army. Arms to Nagorno-Karabakh were supplied by Russian soldiers through Armenia.

The source drew a freehand sketch of the proposed attack, to scale and in some detail suggesting that the plan had been fully and frequently discussed (see right).

The 'operation pipeline' scenario is simple enough: Russia supplies arms to Azerbaijan to provoke it into renewed action against the Nagorno-Karabakh army occupying its terrritory and lets it carry the blame for initiating hostilities. In response, Armenian or Karabakh divisions with excellent training, superior technical equipment and assistance from the Russian army (from its bases in Georgia and Armenia) take the city of Evlakh and advance north to the Ningechaursky reservoir. At the same time, an attack strikes northward from Armenian territory towards the town of Kazakh. Result: the occupation of 12,000 square kilometres and 200 kilometres of pipeline.

Russian military bases in Georgia are on the Black Sea coast at Poti and Batumi, both prospective oil terminals.

BGI news agency

• •

pressure on Karabakh, Armenia and Abkhazia, thus helping Azerbaijan and Georgia to restore their territorial integrity.

Russian policy in Transcaucasia has reached a critical point. Russia faces a dilemma: should it accept the logic of Shevardnadze, Aliyev, Turkey and the West and depart once and for all from Transcaucasia and subsequently from the north Caucasus too (in the wake of Chechnya, Moscow risks losing Ingushetia and Dagestan soon; 'from then on,' as a satirist put it, 'the train will be stopping at all stations'); or should it finally make use of the existing opportunities to maintain its presence and influence in the region?

If the second option is chosen, Russia will have to make strenuous

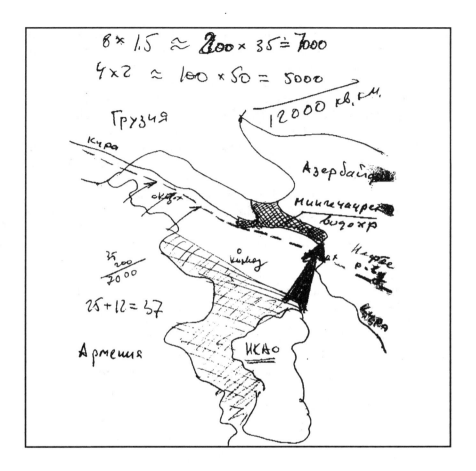

efforts to weaken the position of the anti-Russian forces in Azerbaijan and Georgia and, at the same time, demonstrably strengthen its economic and military-political presence in Armenia before the West and Armenia's neighbours find the money with which to make Yerevan look West.

The blockade of Abkhazia must be lifted immediately. (This is also important for internal political purposes: incentives have to be found to prevent the Russian north Caucasus from uniting on a pro-Chechen basis. Bearing in mind that the Chechen leadership already appreciates the need for a special relationship with Georgia — Chechnya's only external border — lifting the blockade against Abkhazia and then adopting measures to revive the country economically will make it possible to unite the whole of the non-Vainakh north Caucasus around the objectives of Russian policy at the expense of Georgia).

Russia must also promote the strengthening of ties between North and South Ossetia, and encourage the separatist tendencies in Adzharia [Adjaria]. Additionally, Yerevan can be given to understand that, if Georgia continues with its anti-Russian policy, Armenia will be able de facto to absorb the region known as Javakhk in Armenian and Javakheti in Georgian, and subsequently to carve out a corridor providing Armenia with a direct land link with Russia. The threat of such a serious destabilisation of Georgia, backed by a show of Russia's determination to follow this road to the end, would have a sobering effect on the present Georgian leadership.

As for resisting Azerbaijan's efforts to squeeze Russia out of the region, here, too, more effective use must be made of Moscow's resources. First, the Armenian army's military superiority over the Azeri forces should be supported. Second, encouragement should be given to unifying the divided Lezghian people. This would immediately create a new situation in northern Azerbaijan and in Dagestan, which has been experiencing difficult times since the elections in Chechnya. The 'federalisation' of Azerbaijan should be spurred on. Finally, the problem of Talysh autonomy could be stirred up. All these elements must be combined to bring about a situation in which the risk to capital investment in oil production and transportation would be unbearably high.

Apart from Armenia, Iran, too, could be an ally of Russia. Although it has its own interests, Iran may, in view of its internal ethnic problems and its international isolation, confine itself to the role of strategic partner of Russia.

To sum up: as things now stand, only the prospect of destabilisation in Georgia and Azerbaijan can prevent the consolidation of state power in these countries on an anti-Russian basis. Only this can bar the inflow of big money into the region. And only then can Russia's final expulsion from Transcaucasia, and the upsetting of the balance that has been established in this part of the world, be prevented. ❑

Excerpted from the article 'CIS: Beginning or End of History', published in Nezavisimaya Gazeta *26 March 1997*

Translated by Ken Russell

MIKAEL DANIELYAN

Dumbing down

Democracy in Armenia plays second fiddle to the 'great national idea'. Backed by a willing 'patriotic' press, the government has got most dissenting voices nicely stitched up

ARMENIAN President Levon Ter-Petrosyan declares himself well satisfied with the democratic and human rights credentials of his government. His military–political regime has all the attributes of democracy: a colourful and varied political opposition, more than 1,000 non-governmental organisations, a media that declares itself free and independent, even its own share of political prisoners and a president who is, when compared to others in the Commonwealth of Independent States, almost a dissident. Everything else of any significance is guaranteed by the constitution.

But in practice, since rights in Armenia are defined solely in terms of political and nationalist interests, things work out rather differently. Life is hedged by taboos; to mention the unspeakable is, as Armenia's journalists have discovered, to court official reprimand, threats, the loss of a job and, at worst, prison.

In 1995 the Armenian parliament adopted a law to retain Russian military bases on Armenian soil. Of the 149 deputies present, 147, representing all shades of political opinion, voted in favour. Though the fate of 'independent and sovereign Armenia' is intimately linked to the presence — or not — of the Russian bases, the press declined to debate the matter. The most 'independent' paper, the Russian-language *Golos Armenii* (Voice of Armenia), boldly told the authorities that this far-reaching decision should have been taken ages ago. And when, during parliamentary debates on ratification of the treaty, the deputy speaker Ara Sahakyan of the ruling Armenian National Movement dubbed those opposing the treaty 'part of the Jewish lobby', the newspaper *Ayjm* (Now) followed up with an unsigned article headlined 'When the Jews speak, the West listens.'

In 1993, when the Armenian army was fighting on the Karabakh front, the demand for cannon fodder was so pressing that military call-up became a form of terrorism. Those called up for military service were grabbed at home, on the street, on the bus — anywhere. Within days they were on the front line. All of which went on with the tacit approval of the authorities. Only one deputy, the academician Rafael Ishkhanyan (who has since died), called for an end to the terror. The reply of the defence minister, Vazgen Sarkisyan, was characteristic: 'I'm over there seizing land for you and you're not even satisfied. I'll have to come to parliament, round you all up and send you to the front.'

No Armenian paper would touch a piece on this, but it was published in the Russian paper *Ekspress-Khronika* (Express Chronicle). I received a call from the information and press department of Nagorno-Karabakh: 'You call us fascists? Don't forget we have a lot of spare guns and we can easily arrange for you to be sent here to do some shooting yourself.'

In 1995, Dimitry Leonov and Svetlana Ganushkina from Russia and Bernard Klassen from Germany visited Armenia, Azerbaijan and Nagorno-Karabakh. They published a report and a number of articles about what they had seen. Ganushkina's article in *Ekspress-Khronika* annoyed both the authorities and other journalists in Karabakh. The names of the three were added to the list of enemies of the nation.

Vagram Agandjanyan, an official of the information and press department as well as a special correspondent for the Yerevan paper *Azg* (Nation) and for the Armenian service of Radio Liberty (RL), accused Ganushkina of prejudice and pro-Azerbaijani bias. Even this, however, was not enough to save him from the wrath of the Karabakh leadership. Dissatisfied over a series of articles, it detained Agandjanyan, fired him from the information and press department and demanded that the editor of *Azg* and the director of RL's Armenian service do the same. The Armenian service director carried out his orders, telling Agandjanyan: 'When they [the Karabakh leadership] confirm your loyalty to them I'll reinstate you.'

Colleagues on RL's Armenian service were outraged — not by the actions of their director, but by my piece in *Ekspress-Khronika* revealing what had happened in the Agandjanyan case, as well as in that of Vahan Ishkhanyan, a journalist with *Ayjm*, who had, at my request, published an

War in Karabakh 1993: Armenian fighters bury their dead — Credit: David Orr/Panos Pictures

article on the case in *Golos Armenii.*

Agandjanyan's persecution did not stop after the publication of these articles and he was threatened with call-up to the army. His parents appealed to foreign embassies in Yerevan and to human rights organisations, calling on them to protect their son, and I wrote again in *Ekspress-Khronika.* Now it was the turn of the staff of the 'independent' or 'private' news agency Noyan Tapan to express their dissatisfaction. One of them said to me: 'They're very unhappy about your article in Karabakh. Why are you stirring up all this?'

Lusine Oganesyan, a journalist with *Ayjm*, decided to leave the paper after it had printed her piece on Karabakh in June 1996. Her article — the only one I am aware of in the Armenian press to report fully on the state of affairs in Karabakh — unleashed a storm of anger in the Karabakh leadership, in the upper echelons of the National Democratic Union (NDU) — which owns the paper — and among various opposition leaders. Several times that day, the head of the NDU and the joint opposition presidential candidate Vazgen Manukyan personally phoned the Karabakh president, Robert Kocharyan [now prime minister of Armenia — ed], to smooth over the 'misunderstanding'. In the next issue of the paper, in an anonymous statement, *Ayjm*'s chief editor, a member of the Yerevan press club, dissociated himself from Oganesyan's views.

● ●

AVET DEMOURIAN

Fortress Artsakh

The road down the Lachin Corridor — Armenia's sole link with Nagorno-Karabakh — is as perfect as a road can be. In the early morning the cleaners are out sweeping up, brushing away those tiny stones and, apparently, even the dust. After Armenia's roads, unrepaired for seven years and scarred with potholes big enough to swallow a car, it is an impressive sight. But the idyll is over within about 20 kilometres. For the remaining 50 kilometres to the capital of Karabakh, Stepanakert, cars are confined to a track of broken clods of earth with splinters of obsidian, sharp as razors, which tear the tyres to shreds. This section of the road is a round-the-clock work-site: by autumn this year, Armenia and Artsakh (the Armenian name for Karabakh) will be linked by what is, by the standards of the region, a superhighway.

The scale of the project indicates all too clearly that Stepanakert will have no truck with the proposal of the Minsk Group (the OSCE group seeking resolution to the Karabakh problem) to place the Lachin Corridor either under the control of OSCE peace-keeping forces or under Azerbaijani jurisdiction. The OSCE's security guarantees depend heavily on the 'good will' of Azerbaijan, something no-one in Karabakh is prepared to take a chance on. Which is why Karabakh is pinning its hopes on its army.

Karabakh's armed forces are third only to Russia and Ukraine; in military readiness and operational capacity it has no equal. It has a well-functioning hierarchical structure and administration: independent militia groups in the style of the Chechens or the

There are times when I could feel envious of my colleagues' 'scoops'. In April 1994, the parliamentary deputy and writer Vardges Petrosyan was murdered. The interior minister put up a reward of US$10,000 for the capture of his assassins. Suddenly, in July 1996, a sensational newsflash hit TV screens: the murderer had been caught. In the absence of any form of proof, the author's widow, Sona Tigrapyan, was charged with complicity. She spent seven days in the office of the head of the directorate for combating organised crime, followed by three months isolated in the investigation cells of a women's labour camp where they insisted that she should accept the blame for the murder. She was under constant pressure from her cell mates as well as her interrogators. Tigrapyan is today at

Cossacks are unthinkable here. And its operational capacities are currently being built up. Air force divisions have been formed and, according to some sources, tactical missiles have been added.

Karabakh is preparing to defend itself not only, nor even primarily, against Azerbaijan, but in readiness for what many there see as inevitable: the involvement of the international community — the West, NATO and Turkey — in a wide-ranging war. Azerbaijan's contribution to the process, observers in Karabakh maintain, will be to distribute oil concessions, in the face of which principles such as the right of nations to self-determination become irrelevant.

The transformation of Karabakh into an impregnable fortress, the storming of which would bring unacceptable losses to the opposing side, is nearing completion. Regional strongholds, formed round existing administrative districts and reminiscent of the traditional Cossack *stanitsa* at the time of the Caucasian wars in earlier centuries, or of a *kibbutz* in the early years of Israel's existence, have a well-developed system of defensive fortifications and an armed garrison formed from the local population. Each is capable of extended military action — both defensive and offensive — independent of the regular armed forces.

The system guarantees a high level of military preparedness: 10,000-12,000 of a population of 150,000 serve in the army and, should the need arise, 45,000-50,000 reservists with military experience could be instantly mobilised.

Avet Demourian is an Armenian journalist
Translated by Irena Maryniak

● ●

liberty awaiting a trial which will probably never take place.

Throughout this time, the press remained silent. No-one wrote that before her arrest they had kidnapped her son and, before that, had tried to seize her grandson. The lawyers Ruben Sahakyan and Ruben Rshtuni refused to defend her. The Russian paper *Komsomolskaya Pravda* published an article on Tigrapyan by its Yerevan correspondent, Vardan Aloyan, in September 1996. Only later, on being asked why he had not checked his facts before writing, did he admit, 'honestly and truthfully' that the article had been written 'under orders'.

One of the biggest political outrages followed the demonstrations against the results of the 1996 presidential elections at which the authorities opened fire on the thousands of demonstrators who had gathered outside the parliament building in central Yerevan to protest against the ballot-rigging. The president, the minister of the interior and national security and the general procurator all issued statements threatening the opposition. Most characteristic were the remarks of the defence minister, Vazgen Sarkisyan: 'Even if the opposition had won one hundred per cent of the votes, we still wouldn't have handed over power to them.' The opposition and the independent media protested, but went silent when Kocharyan joined the officials in condemning the street protests, claiming that instability in Armenia would threaten the young Karabakh republic. Karabakh and all that pertains to it is above criticism.

The media rarely take up human rights violations even when these touch members of their own fraternity. The beating up of two journalists of the news agency of the Self-Determination Union inside the parliament building in 1992 went unreported; as did the army call-up in 1992-93, the continuing military service by Armenian citizens in Nagorno-Karabakh and occupied territories of Azerbaijan and the mass call-up into the national army of Armenian refugees from Azerbaijan even though they are not citizens of Armenia. The media has been equally silent on the terror unleashed against religious minorities in April 1995 organised by units of the *Erkrapah* (Guardians of the Fatherland), a paramilitary organisation under the direct control of the minister of defence and licensed to carry arms. On the contrary, *Molorak* (Planet), wrote in its columns earlier this year: 'Today the healthy and sane forces of the nation — the writers, artists and scholars — are forced to demand a legal ban on activity by sects (the term for religious minorities). Otherwise, the generation to come will consider the law [on freedom of conscience] not as freedom of conscience but as renunciation and betrayal.' Hot on this, the parliamentary Commission for Questions of Science, Education, Culture and Youth introduced amendments to the law on freedom of conscience which will legalise the onslaught on religious minorities. The chairman of the commission is Rafael Papayan, a member of the ruling Armenian National Movement, a doctor of philology — and a former political prisoner of the Soviet regime. ❏

Mikael Danielyan is chairman of the Armenian Helsinki Association and a correspondent for Ekspress-Khronika
Translated by Felix Corley

INTERVIEWS

IVANE MERABISHVILI

Georgia on my mind

Many see southern Georgia as a potential flashpoint. A Georgian journalist talks to some of its people

Vladimir Karapetyan, aged 34, is a warrant officer in the Russian army guarding the Turkish border with Georgia and Armenia.

Ivane Merabishvili *As a Georgian citizen, an ethnic Armenian and a soldier in the Russian army, don't you find yourself facing conflicting loyalties?*

No...no... Russian border troops guard just one border, that of the CIS. Defence from the threat of an Islamic onslaught is in the interest of all three nations — Armenians, Georgians and Russians. Bearing in mind that Turkey is a member of NATO, we could never deal with an attack alone.

The idea of CIS-assisted defence from the Islamic world sounds odd to me. There are several Muslim states within the CIS; a third of the Russian population is Muslim; and Russia has quite good relations with some Islamic countries, like Iran for instance.

Armenians and Georgians should take advantage of the presence of Russian troops in the Caucasus. History has shown that the ancient Christian peoples of Georgia and Armenia have always suffered from the Islamic world.

But the fact is that Georgia has declared a strategic partnership with Turkey as well as Armenia and Azerbaijan. Furthermore, Turkey and Azerbaijan are Georgia's main trading partners, and part of Georgia is Muslim. I rather doubt that Georgia will want to come into conflict with Islam.

That is Georgia's mistake. Georgia is betraying her historical tradition. Confrontation with Russia will do her no good. On the contrary: that is why Georgia lost Abkhazia and Ossetia. Georgia will never join NATO, as the Georgians like to imagine. NATO has no need of Georgia, and Russia would never allow it anyway. The departure of Russian troops from this country would be a real tragedy. I hope it doesn't happen. If Russian troops leave Georgia and Armenia, they'll both be wiped off the map.

So how do you see your future? Do you think that in 2010 you'll be the citizen of a state (Georgia, Armenia or Russia), or of a regional union like the CIS, or even perhaps the European Union?

That's a tricky question. I think about it sometimes but I don't have a ready answer. Perhaps we'll emigrate. If Russian troops leave Akhalkalaki, I'll be out of a job. It's very hard earning a living here. I can't let my family go hungry. So we'll have to go to Russia. You can get work there and it's much easier to feed a family.

Aslan Beridze, aged 47 and born in Adjaria, is a Georgian Muslim. In 1989, following landslides in High Adjaria he was given state help to move to Javakheti along with several hundred other families.

You came from Adjaria in 1989 but you say you don't live here all the time?

I generally spend the winter at home in Adjaria and live here the rest of the year. Our movements are determined by the elements. The landslide destroyed much of our land and continues to threaten our homes. Even though we have lived here in Dzhavakhety for seven or eight years we don't lose touch with our home. We find life very hard here in winter; it's tough here anyway. There's more workable land here than at home, but there are no trees. It's an alpine region and you can only grow wheat and potatoes. We have to buy the rest if we don't bring it over from our old vegetable gardens in Adjaria.

Apologies for the next question: as you know, this interview is for European readers. You are a Georgian and Muslim; traditionally Georgians are viewed as Christians. Where do you stand on this issue?

Georgia 1997: 'Life is better again, now' — *Credit: Guram Tsibakhashvili*

I am a Muslim and I'm bringing up my children as Muslims. My father and grandfather were Muslims; so are most of my friends and relations. But I'm as much a Georgian as anyone. There are several million Georgians in Turkey and they are Muslims too. I've never felt uncomfortable with Christian friends. There is a fine Georgian saying: 'Be a good man and pray where you please.'

Most of the population of Javakheti is Armenian. At present, the Armenians are in conflict with Azerbaijan over Nagorno-Karabakh. Armenians often view Adjarians negatively, as people with Turkish sympathies. Do you sense this from your neighbours?

Sometimes... But a real Armenian, like any real human being, will set little store by faith or nationality. In the Soviet Union we lived in peace for decades. It seems to me that conflicts are useful to politicians and business people. They score points and earn big money through them. But I still believe the conflicts will end soon and we will live in peace again, as we did once.

Do you think the conflicts were caused by the collapse of the Soviet Union?

Perhaps. In Soviet times we had order and discipline. The state didn't permit ethnic discrimination. We were all equal and things were fine.

Do you think the Soviet Union should be reinstated for things to improve?

The people in power now have nothing to gain from peace. They are making a fortune out of all this. The CIS doesn't change a thing. The people in power today don't think in terms of human beings. And the conflicts began in Russia itself. Russian politicians are not in the least embarrassed to kill thousands of people in Chechnya. We're unlikely to achieve anything until we recognise that we need peace above everything.

Martiros Sapondzhyan, aged 38, is an Armenian, living in the Akhaltsikhsky region.

How would you describe the situation in Georgia today?

Life's improving. Two years ago it was much harder. It's very fashionable now to remember Communism and the Soviet era, but people still had to work. The state helped everyone, or rather anyone who asked for it. People grew accustomed to not working and now they complain that life's hard. The Soviet Union collapsed because it helped everyone, including foreign states.

Do you feel a full Georgian citizen?

Why not? My ancestors lived here and I hope my children will as well. I am an Armenian and I feel for Armenia, but Georgia is my country. All my friends and relations live here, I was educated here, I know Georgia's language and culture better than Armenia's.

Occasions may arise when Georgian and Armenian interests clash. For example, Georgia is more inclined to co-operation with the West; Armenia looks to Russia; Armenia is in conflict with Azerbaijan and Georgia is building close relations with it.

I have my own views on the Nagorno–Karabakh conflict. When the war was at its height, friends suggested that I join up. I said to them: 'I've never been to Karabakh and I'll probably never go. I know that in the past Armenians and Azeris from Karabakh had excellent relations. They intermarried. Why should I start killing men who, only recently, would have been regarded as perfectly good husbands for the daughters of Karabakh Armenians?' A lot of people disagreed and went to fight. Many never returned and their children are now orphaned. And what of it? Karabakh is now controlled by Armenians, and so what? For how long? The Azeris will gather power and renew the war and so it will go on. These days nobody wins wars.

If the Georgian government were to call you up to fight an 'enemy' would your position be the same?

Broadly speaking, yes. I'll only take up arms if my family is at risk or if the 'enemy' is threatening my friends. Then I'll fight. But I'd hate to have to do it. ❏

Ivane Merabishvili *is a journalist working in Tbilisi*

Translated by Irena Maryniak

GENNADY ZHAVORONKOV

War of words

The Abkhazian-Georgian conflict began in the pages of the press long before it erupted into full-blown civil war. Even now, despite a fragile peace, the media is up to its old tricks

Tbilisi, Georgia: wayside gallery, of missing persons — Credit: J C Tordai/Panos Pictures

THERE is nothing new about the hostility between Georgia and Abkhazia: whenever the opportunity presented itself, as in 1783, or the Civil War that followed the 1917 revolution, the two neighbours found themselves on opposite sides and at each other's throats. In the 1920s, Stalin forcibly joined Abkhazia to Georgia and there was a renewed spate of hostilities.

By the 1950s, the Georgian population outnumbered the Abkhazian and unarmed war was declared over issues vital to the latter such as the survival of schools teaching their language and their university.

It was a hard-fought battle which the Abkhazians eventually won.

And there matters stood until the media decided to enter the fray. Despite the emergence of a growing number of Abkhazian newspapers — chief among them *Respublika Abkhazii* (Republic of Abkhazia), *Bzyb* and *Aydgylara* (Unity), the organ of the Popular Front — the Georgians invariably emerged triumphant in an endless succession of verbal skirmishes over the future of the two entities. Georgian journalists labelled their opponents separatist Communists and were, in turn, accused of fascism; the Georgians claimed the Abkhazians were newcomers who espoused Islam; the Abkhazians that there were many millions of Abkhazians in Turkey ready to descend on the lands of their forefathers. The press assumed an even more active role by mobilising its supporters in rival rallies and demonstrations.

The Russian media remained silent and the population of the former USSR largely ignorant of a conflict that was, as yet, only slightly bloody.

'What are those rallies going on down there?' Russian holiday-makers on the Black Sea coast asked anxiously. And back came the soothing reply: 'Well, they're a minority people and like to make a fuss. Sometimes they want Abkhazian schools, at other times they're after a university. Why do they need all that when they haven't even got a language of their own?'

No historical works on Abkhazia were being printed, and most Russians was happy to go along with the mythology claiming that the Abkhazians were some newly arrived people who had just come down from the mountains and had had the effrontery to settle on the coast. In any case, weren't they all Muslims and keen to annihilate Christians?

In 1985, *perestroika* enabled the first breach in the information blackout. When Abkhazian scholars began to publish historical works on their people, Russians were surprised to discover an unfamiliar and unique culture that had survived despite the harsh vicissitudes of the past.

There are no Abkhazian Muslims; they are mostly pagans, worshipping the earth, the sun and the vine, to which the human soul is thought to migrate. They bury their dead in their own courtyards and are loud in their lamentations. Later, they talk to them as though they were alive, pour libations of wine onto the grave and put out bread for the dead. All their songs are sad. They enter easily into mixed marriages and are wholly tolerant of their numerous foreign neighbours — Russians, Armenians, Estonians and Jews. Their only antipathy is for the Georgians who persist in calling them visitors in their own land.

There was never slavery nor serfdom in Abkhazia. Love of the earth is central to Abkhazians' religion and those who remain in Abkhazia know that though those who fled to Turkey gained in material wealth, they never attained spiritual peace. Their souls remain here, in this land, which they wish to repossess.

The local Gagra newspaper *Bzyb* filled its pages with these historical treatises and the Georgian press counter-attacked.

The Georgian paper *Abkhazia* tried, to no avail, to steer a median and moderating course through the storm, warning of the dangerous passions that the press was unleashing. But once the Georgian-held town of Sukhumi had been occupied by the Abkhazian irregulars, the newspaper's editor-in-chief, Yuri Gavba, was arrested, accused of inciting ethnic conflict. He spent almost a year in prison. His life was saved by the intervention of international human rights organisations, but up to 40 journalists on both sides were killed or went missing. And still the flood of disinformation, now allied to calls for the rebellious 'Muslims' to be suppressed, found its way into the pages of the Georgian press.

Everyone expected war but persuaded themselves it could not happen. But this is the land of the blood feud: grievances in the Caucasus are inherited.

And war did break out. The guards of the self-styled Georgian commander Tengiz Kitovani launched a sudden tank offensive against Abkhazia intending to restore 'law and order'. It began like a military parade — an unopposed advance into the middle of Abkhazia, shots fired into the air. Then came the resistance; both sides fought with the heavy guns and Grad multiple rocket launchers they had inherited from the USSR. The defeated Georgian irregulars fled, accompanied by many thousands of Georgian-speaking civilians.

The whole world tried to help douse the flames of war and resolve the seemingly intractable conflict in Yugoslavia. With the exception of Russia, the Georgian–Abkhazian war went unnoticed.

Today, despite a fragile peace, newspapers continue their implacable information war, accusing each other of atrocities. Not so long ago, *Georgia* published a map showing concentration camps and supposed training camps for Chechen guerrillas in Abkhazia. I toured these 'locations' with the peacekeeping forces and found nothing. The paper decided not to challenge my findings. The Abkhazians, too, on occasion, launch into shrill protest. Both sides still accuse each other of inhuman

● ●

From the onset of hostilities, the Russian media began their own information war, some unreservedly backing Georgia, deemed to be a staunch fighter against separatists, others the Abkhazians, seen as resisting an aggressor. Volunteers hastened to swell the conflagration and laid down their lives in considerable numbers

● ●

cruelty — football matches with severed heads, women and children shut up in sewers, scarecrows made of corpses.

Finally, only this year, Russia's human rights movement persuaded Abkhazian and Georgian journalists to sit down at a negotiating table in Moscow where they adopted a joint declaration bringing the media war to an end. Shortly after, a news story came in from Georgia and was run by all the media: civil war had begun in Abkhazia, arms dumps were exploding, and President Vladislav Ardzinba had been toppled by the opposition. I was able to find out in a matter of hours that it was yet another piece of disinformation, one with potentially disastrous consequences. The media war had resumed. ❏

Gennady Zhavoronkov, *a journalist working for* Obshchaya Gazeta, *Moscow, travelled to Abkhazia for* Dos'e na Tsenzuru

Translated by Ken Russell

AYAZ AKHMEDOV

Notes of an accused man

Ayaz Akhmedov, editor of the satirical newspaper *Cheshma* (Spring) was put on trial in Baku from 3-19 October 1995 with three other journalists. He was found guilty under article 188-6 part 2 of the Criminal Code of the Azerbaijan Republic — 'Insulting the honour and dignity of the president of the republic through the mass media' — and was sentenced to five years' imprisonment. On 11 November of the same year he was pardoned and released from custody by decree of President Heydar Aliyev

JUDGE *(reading out the submission for the prosecution)*: ... thus it has been proved that the items of evidence 'Muddled bureaucrats for the president's authoritarian lust'

Laughter in court

JUDGE Silence! *(continues reading)*... 'five fig leaves for the Summit of naked kings', 'Acting crazy, scum?!', 'Lawmaker's striptease'...

Laughter in court

JUDGE Be quiet, what's funny about this! *(continues reading)* ...'An epidemic of philological dysentery in parliament', 'The president's half-ear, two mouths and dozen fists', 'Heydar Aliyev forced to marry the opposition'...

Loud laughter in court

JUDGE What is the meaning of this continual laughter?!

COUNSEL FOR THE DEFENCE You are reading something funny so we are laughing, Your Honour.

JUDGE You should be crying, not laughing! *(continues reading)* and also the cartoon with the title: 'Comrade Ragimzade, I've told you that if you have arthritis'...

Laughter in court

JUDGE Silence at once! *(continues reading)* '... if you have arthritis, you don't have to bow'...

Increasing laughter in court

JUDGE Silence! Guards, remove that man in the tie from the court! Not that one, what are you doing, he works for the KGB, I mean that one on the left! No, not that one, further to the right!

FROM THE COURT Just remove all the men wearing ties and get it over with!

Uproar, laughter, whistles in court

★ ★ ★

DEFENCE *(question to the counsel for the prosecution)* You assert that the newspaper *Cheshma* belongs to the mass media. The law defines mass media as an edition of not less than 1,000 copies. How can you prove that a minimum of 1,000 copies of each edition of *Cheshma* was published? The editor states that no issue of the newspaper exceeded 500 copies. Do you have as proof one thousand copies of any edition of this newspaper?

PROSECUTION Here on the last page of the newspaper it states... I quote:

'The size of the edition corresponds to the number of hairs on Arif Ragimadze's head', end of quote. Is it your opinion that I should count the hairs on the parliamentary deputy speaker's head in order to determine the size of the edition of this delinquent newspaper?!

★ ★ ★

EXPERT WITNESS It is the height of shamelessness and blasphemy when a newspaper mocks the very fact that a 70-year-old atheist repents and goes on a pilgrimage to the holy places of Islam.

DEFENCE Allow me! Who is this atheist but our dear president?! What on earth are you saying?!

EXPERT WITNESS So in your opinion a person who works for 30 years for the KGB and leads the Communist Party for 15 years is a pious man?

JUDGE Comrade Expert Witness, I would ask you to be extremely cautious in your choice of words...

★ ★ ★

AKHMEDOV Mister Expert Witness...

EXPERT WITNESS Don't you call me mister!

AKHMEDOV Well, you're not a comrade, though unfortunately you may very well become my comrade if the court finds me guilty in this instance. You too would have to share my guilt in that case, wouldn't you?

EXPERT WITNESS For what reason?

AKHMEDOV Don't you understand? For reading forbidden literature! These young people are sitting on the accused bench with me simply because they read *Cheshma*.

EXPERT WITNESS But I haven't read this damned *Cheshma*...

AKHMEDOV In that case how can you as an expert witness determine that the material contains insults or in general whether it is, as you just expressed it, 'damned'?

EXPERT WITNESS The prosecution office submitted a prepared document, the rector of the university assented and told our comrades that one should help and I signed... Is there something in the criminal code that applies to that? I swear to you that I have not read a single line of this newspaper!

AKHMEDOV Ahah! In that case you are threatened by a more serious punishment: submitting faked expert evidence which is an act far more severely punishable than reading subversive literature.

EXPERT WITNESS But I... You... You guttersnipe!... Your Honour, I don't understand who's on trial here: me or them?

Laughter in court

JUDGE Quiet! Akhmedov, you are getting up to your old tricks again. What do you think this is, a courtroom or a circus?!

★ ★ ★

AKHMEDOV My dear expert witness, how do you explain the fact that you were the one they asked to assess the value of my newspaper?

EXPERT WITNESS I have a specialist training!

AKHMEDOV Do you have any academic qualifications?

EXPERT WITNESS Of course — I have a doctorate and am a lecturer in the faculty of journalism!

AKHMEDOV Ah, that's marvellous! If it's no secret, may I ask the subject of your dissertation and your research speciality?

EXPERT WITNESS What does this have to do with the matter in hand?

AKHMEDOV Exactly as much as this portrait of the president in the court has to do with justice. So in what terms do you describe the subject of your work?

EXPERT WITNESS I don't have to describe anything! I do not wish to reply to your stupid question, and stop pestering me!

DEFENCE Gentlemen, allow me to reply on behalf of our worthy expert witness. Out of modesty he is evidently embarrassed to speak aloud about his own achievements. His subject is as follows: 'THE ORGANISATION OF PARTY WORK ON COLLECTIVE FARMS AND STATE FARMS'.

AKHMEDOV *loudly:* Where did you say that was? I didn't hear the end, could you please repeat?

DEFENCE *loudly* On collective farms and state farms, Akhmedov.

AKHMEDOV *loudly:* On collective farms and state farms?

DEFENCE *loudly* Yes, Akhmedov, on collective farms and state farms.

AKHMEDOV Could I just confirm what sort of organisation it was?

DEFENCE Of party work.

Uproar and loud laughter in court

A QUESTION FROM THE COURTROOM What party is that?

FROM THE COURTROOM Probably 'the heavy drinkers' party'...

JUDGE Silence! Akhmedov, be silent! Quiet! These circus antics must cease!!! The court is adjourned!

★ ★ ★

AKHMEDOV I naturally admit that a certain contradiction is to be found in the newspaper *Cheshma* between the semantic stress on the published word combinations and any question of merit. But in your expert witness statement why do you classify the word 'WOLF' as an insulting expression?

EXPERT WITNESS In literature any parallel between people and animals is classified as an insulting attack, especially if one is speaking of the president. That applies to any, whether dog or rat, swine, ass, fox and so on.

AKHMEDOV But excuse me, Mister Expert Witness...

EXPERT WITNESS Don't call me mister!

AKHMEDOV But why are you taking offence, surely 'mister' is not a zoological term? Let us look at your final example of an animal — the fox. *Cheshma* bestowed the honour of this title upon the former parliamentary speaker Isa Gambarov. I will give you the exact quote: 'The meeting was attended by Fox...sorry...Isa Gambarov'.* I, as the author of the text in question, would go so far as to affirm that this is a compliment rather than an insult. After all the fox is a symbol of craftiness. And you must admit that craftiness is an utterly essential quality in politics. Why are you staring at me as if you'd met somebody from outer space? Just take a look round: people use endearments for their own children and call them 'my little shrimp', 'my pussycat', 'my bunny rabbit'. Do you think they are insulting their own offspring?! Surely you too were called 'little mite' or 'little mouse' as a child...

Laughter in court

DEFENCE Respected expert witness, I would like to ask you a question in order to demonstrate to Ayaz the point of continuing a discussion of this topic. Do you know what a METAPHOR is?

EXPERT WITNESS Is it some Greek philosopher?

AKHMEDOV Many thanks, mister defence, you have certainly helped me greatly.

* * *

AKHMEDOV Could you tell me why you arrested Asker?

PROSECUTION Obviously because he was distributing *Cheshma*, indecent literature...

AKHMEDOV You consider that this is sufficient grounds to arrest an academic and teacher, one of the leaders of the country's largest political party, and to keep him for months without trial in the KGB solitary confinement cells?

PROSECUTION Without doubt. The law does not specify who it is that is distributing *samizdat*, whether it is a vagrant or a doctor of philosophy — everyone has the same responsibilities.

AKHMEDOV In that case let me be the first to gratefully offer some evidence and I would ask that it should be included in these criminal proceedings.

Among the video cassettes taken from my apartment by members of the KGB on 2 March 1995 there were scenes of members of our parliament handing each other *Cheshma* — during the course of a session of the supreme lawmaking body of the republic. In what way is that not distribution? Arrest the members of parliament. There is only one witnessed deposition against Asker and that is given by a person who has spent three-quarters of his life in psychiatric hospitals. Against the members of parliament there are video films as well as my frank confession...

JUDGE Akhmedov! I am tired of asking you to be serious...

AKHMEDOV I beg your pardon, since when have parliament and its members wandered off into the sphere of jokes?... As I understand it, you and I may not touch members of parliament: our arms are too short, so to speak.

My dear prosecutor! How many copies did you say that Asker distributed?

PROSECUTOR At least 19 items.

AKHMEDOV You mean copies. Newspapers are not lemons, they are not measured by item...

I will present to you a fact whose truth may easily be verified. It is to do with the mass distribution of my newspaper. As a minimum there were 250-300 copies, if not more. May I, Your Honour?

JUDGE Well... I suppose so... carry on. But would you please stick to the subject.

AKHMEDOV On 1 March 1995 members of the Ministry of Internal Affairs conducted a thorough search of the headquarters of the National Front of Azerbaijan [NFA]. Among the many pieces of criminal evidence (military rations, cartridges, Molotov cocktails) the detectives discovered several packets of fresh copies of *Cheshma* intended for distribution among supporters of the organisation. The fact of the discovery of the newspapers and their quantity is recorded in the report. There is evidence with all the legal formalities. But that is not all. The NFA building was sealed up and the evidence transported to the premises of the Sabail borough department of the Baku police force. Within a day there was not a single copy of the newspaper left in the room where the police had stored them. The reason for the mysterious disappearance of almost half the edition of *Cheshma* was explained to me with a smile by the duty officer (there is a recording

of this confession): 'All our colleagues took a copy or two each, to take them home to his family or neighbours for a laugh. One major from a neighbouring department drove here specially to get some copies for himself. I myself took three, I'll take them to the country with me to cheer them up.' As you see, the entire staff of a department of a vital ministry of this country appears in the role of my collaborators in what you have termed my crime. Your Honours, prove that you have arrested Asker specifically for distributing *Cheshma* and not, as the newspapers say, for belonging to the opposition. Prove that, as far as you are concerned, criminals have no party membership! On the one hand an active member of the 'Musavat' party supposedly distributes a paltry 19 copies, on the other hand agents of the law with epaulettes, an entire department, distributes hundreds of newspapers throughout the country. Put the head of this police department on the accused bench. We can squeeze him in with us. Demonstrate your impartiality!

JUDGE Akhmedov, stop turning this court into a political gathering! Be quiet!!! ❏

Translated by Michael Molnar
Illustrations by Jan Brychta

*Translator's footnote: Word-play on Lisa (fox) and Isa

INDEX INDEX

Democratic deceptions

G IVEN the number of elections that have taken place in recent weeks, the casual observer might be forgiven for thinking that democracy had broken out around the world. Countries as diverse as Algeria, Canada, Croatia, France, Indonesia, Iran, Ireland, Mongolia and the United Kingdom all sent voters to the polls to exercise their democratic rights in May and June. Congo (Brazzaville) — in a state of violent but undeclared civil war as we go to press — Albania and Mexico are shortly to follow suit.

What this rash of ballots proves, if anything, is that this is a far more complicated thing than simply choosing a government. In extreme cases, such as Indonesia, it's more of a ritual sanctification of the existing power arrangements for the benefit of the outside world. With the ruling coalition, Golkar, certain to win, the only question of psephological interest was how big the opposition vote would be. In the end, the opposition parties (both sanctioned by the government) didn't do nearly so well as the abstentions. According to the Independent Election Monitoring Committee (KIPP) in Jakarta, 30 per cent of the electorate either did not turn up to vote, spoilt their ballot papers, or turned up but left their papers blank. In Bali the protest vote was second only to the Golkar vote.

Similarly Algeria's parliamentary election wasn't so much about constituting a government that would be acceptable to the people as constituting an opposition that would be acceptable to the government. The National Democratic Rally, which supports President Zeroual, won with predictable ease amid allegations, supported by international observers, of massive vote-rigging in several areas. Here too voter turnout was low, indicating that many had heeded the call by the Islamic Salvation Front (FIS) for a boycott. Since by rights it is the FIS which should be in government — having been poised for victory in the last election, before the army annulled the results — their absence from the campaign made the whole process nugatory. And so the violence continues, particularly in rural areas, where there has been a post-election upsurge in reports of dawn massacres, village burnings and throat-cuttings. No amount of bal-lot-stuffing is going to make that kind of brutality go away.

Albania is another case of elections being used as a sticking-plaster solution to a profound social and political crisis. At the time of writing, the Organisation for Security and Co-operation in Europe seems more determined than ever to press ahead with the vote as scheduled on 29 June, despite the lack of infrastructure, poor communications, the spi-ralling violence (over 1,500 people killed so far this year) and virtual mob rule in the south. The OSCE's warning that only those of 'strong mental and physical disposition' should apply to join the monitoring team was borne out in the southern town of Gjirokaster in mid-June, when 11 for-eign monitors were taken hostage in a restaurant by a group of armed men demanding money with menaces.

But there's a brighter side to this election business, as evidenced by Mohammad Khatami's surprise landslide victory in Iran's presidential election in May. Support for the moderate former culture minister came largely from women, the young, the rural poor and the intellectuals, all of them united in a desire for change. Even Ayatollah Khamenei, the coun-try's conservative spiritual leader who had, up to the election, endorsed the hard-line favourite, *majlis* speaker Mohammed Nateq-Nouri, was moved to greet Khatami's win with the declaration that 'a shining point for change has appeared in our history.' Given that he must work with a parliament that retains its conservative character, however, it will be hard for Khatami to satisfy the wave of optimism and expectation that swept him into office. So let's add one more appeal to the clamour for good measure: that he immediately and unconditionally order the release of the detained editor Faraj Sarkoohi. Then we might really have cause to believe in the healing power of the ballot box. ❑

Adam Newey, formerly news editor at Index, *has recently joined the* New Statesman

A censorship chronicle incorporating information from the American Association for the Advancement of Science Human Rights Action Network (AAASHRAN), Amnesty International (AI), Article 19 (A19), the BBC Monitoring Service Summary of World Broadcasts (SWB), the Committee to Protect Journalists (CPJ), the Canadian Committee to Protect Journalists (CCPJ), the Inter-American Press Association (IAPA), the International Federation of Journalists (IFJ/FIP), the International Press Institute (IPI), the International Federation of Newspaper Publishers (FIEJ), Human Rights Watch (HRW), the Media Institute of Southern Africa (MISA), the Network for the Defence of Independent Media in Africa (NDIMA), International PEN (PEN), Radio Free Europe/Radio Liberty (RFE/RL), Reporters Sans Frontières (RSF), the World Organisation Against Torture (OMCT) and other sources

ALBANIA

The 27 April edition of the independent daily *Koha Jone* was banned because of a report on popular calls for daily demonstrations in the Vlora area. Officials said that the article violated emergency measures imposed to quell unrest. (RFE/RL)

The weekly *Bashkimi* resumed publication on 17 May after a three-month suspension. Two days later its offices were raided and all its computer equipment was stolen, forcing it to stop publishing again. On 20 May the Albanian Journalists' Union

issued a statement protesting against continued harassment of much of the press. In particular, the Union criticised the so-called 'salvation committees' that have prevented the distribution of independent and right-wing newspapers in the south of the country. Delivery vehicles for the papers *Albania* and *Rilindja* have regularly been burned and journalists and technical staff abused. (SWB)

Eight people were wounded during a shoot-out at a Democratic Party campaign rally in Elbasan on 12 June. Presidential guards reportedly fired on hecklers in the crowd who were making anti-Berisha taunts. Armed men then fired back on the guards, killing at least three of them. On 18 June a group of armed men stopped a Socialist Party convoy on the way to the town of Rreshen and refused to allow party leader Fatos Nano to hold a rally there. A meeting was finally held, but without Nano. (RFE/RL)

ALGERIA

Recent publication: *Elections in the Shadow of Violence and Repression* (HRW/Middle East, June 1997, 35pp)

ARMENIA

Kim Balayan, a member of the Dashnak party, was given a two-year suspended sentence in early June on charges of inciting mass disturbances. Five other defendants, also tried for their role in the attack on parliament last September (*Index* 6/1996), were granted amnesties on 5 June

after being sentenced to between 18 and 30 months' imprisonment. (RFE/RL)

Reporter Jeanna Grigorieva, executive director Tigran Harutiunian and editor-in-chief Gayaneh Arakelian of Noyan Tapan were interrogated by the Ministry of National Security on 18 June. They were accused of spying after the agency distributed an unsigned article on the Karabakh issue. (RSF)

AUSTRALIA

Editors of student magazine *Rabelais* are facing criminal proceedings after the Federal Court, on 6 June, dismissed an appeal against the Review Board banning of the July 1995 edition. An article entitled 'The Art of Shoplifting' lead to federal funding of the magazine being cut and the arrest of all four editors for inciting or instructing crime. If convicted the defendants face up to six years in gaol or US$54,000 in fines. (Students Defence Committee)

AZERBAIJAN

On 7 June Kamil Ali, correspondent with the Sharg agency and the weekly *Zerkalo*, was assaulted and forcibly removed from the parliament hall by a guard who accused him of speaking too loudly. After the remaining journalists walked out in solidarity, the guard concerned offered an apology. (*Ekspress-Khronika*)

BAHRAIN

Sixty-six people were detained between late April

and mid-June in a fresh government assault on the opposition movement. They are believed to have been detained after participating in peaceful anti-government demonstrations in Daih and Sanabis. (Bahrain Human Rights Organisation)

On 14 June Shi'ite Muslims **Hassan Qassab, Shaker al-Mahouzi, Mirza al-Qatari, Saleh Hassan, Ali Isa Ahmed** and **Hussain Howaida** were convicted of possessing illegal leaflets, said to contain false news and unfounded statements. All six were promptly released having already spent 14 months in gaol. (Reuters)

BELARUS

The authorities continued their crackdown on unauthorised demonstrations. Those punished include opposition activists **Viktar Kraniyenka**, chairman of the United Civic Party, and **Uladzimar Starchanka**, chairman of the Belarusian Popular Front, who were each fined US$850 for organising a commemorative rally on the anniversary of the Chernobyl disaster; and **Nikolai Statkevich**, leader of the Belarusian Social Democratic Party, gaoled for 10 days on 2 May for organising an unsanctioned opposition rally. This was Statkevich's third arrest in six months. Meanwhile the organisers of an unauthorised youth procession in Minsk on 14 May, **Ales Chekholsky** and **Nikolai Antsipovich**, and a participant **Vitaly Umreyko**, an observer from the Belarusian Helsinki Committee, were also detained and charged. In

mid-May former members of the disbanded parliament **Semyon Sharetsky, Valery Shchukin** and **Anatoly Lebedko** were fined for their part in an illegal demonstration held in Minsk on 15 March. Shchukin, who organised the protest, was fined US$850, while Sharetsky and Lebedko were each fined US$190. (RFE/RL, AI, SWB)

President Lukashenka announced on 7 May his intention to tighten government control of academic appointments. The institutes of history and economics were both criticised for destabilising the country and university bodies warned to 'get rid of husk and scum'. (SWB)

The **Soros Foundation** (*Index* 3/1997) suspended its activities in Belarus in mid-May after almost US$3 million in fines was sequestered from its bank account. Tax officials had charged the organisation with administering grants in violation of its charitable status. (*Financial Times*, RFE/RL)

On 14 June **Slavamir Adamovich** (*Index* 4/1996) was found guilty of writing and distributing a poem, 'Kill the President', deemed to have insulted a state official. Having already served the length of his 14-month sentence in detention, he was released, but is still liable for court expenses and the cost of translating the poem from Belarusian into Russian. (SWB)

BELGIUM

On 17 June Bruges police

searched and confiscated material from the office of *De Morgen* journalist **Hans Van Scharen**. Van Scharen, who is covering the so-called 'hormone mafia' case, is accused of possessing documents from judicial sources. Four days later the homes of six other journalists — **Josse Abrahams** and **Georges Timmerma** of *De Morgen*, **Danny Ilegems** and **Raf Sauviller** of *Humo* and **Paul Keysers** and **Eric Goens**, formerly of *Panorama De Post* — were also searched in connection with several legal cases. (RSF)

BOSNIA-HERCEGOVINA

Police in Sarajevo confiscated all copies of the satirical Tuzla bi-weekly *Politika* on 5 June. The cover had a photomontage of Alija Izetbegovic, chairman of the collective presidency, metamorphosing into Marshal Tito, with the caption 'After Tito — Tito'. Street vendors reported receiving threatening phone calls and were summoned for questioning by the police, who accused them of not having a licence to sell the paper. (Institute for War and Peace Reporting, Reuters)

Election monitors in Sarajevo closed all four voter registration offices in Brcko on 11 June because of gross irregularities by the Bosnian Serb authorities. Local elections due to be held across Bosnia last year were postponed until September 1997 because of massive registration fraud, especially by the Serbs. Each of the three sides has registered voters in such a way as to consolidate its hold over key territories. (RFE/RL)

Recent publication: *From Promise to Reality* (AI, June 1997, 9pp)

BOTSWANA

On 28 May the Botswanan army stopped the sale of the privately owned newspaper the *Gazette* on one of its barracks after the paper ran a story about allegations that the army commander, Lieutenant General Ian Khama, operated the defence force as a family business. The same day the government announced a draft bill to regulate all media. Under the proposals the police will be empowered to seize any publication deemed to contravene the law, foreign journalists will require accreditation and foreign ownership of the media is to be limited to 20 per cent. (MISA)

BRAZIL

Recent publication: *Candelaria and Vigario Geral — Justice at a Snail's Pace* (AI, June 1997, 9pp)

BULGARIA

The head of the Bulgarian Orthodox Church, **Patriarch Maxim**, filed a complaint with the European Human Rights Commission against the Supreme Court and the prosecutor general in early May. The Patriarch is protesting the Court's decision in July last year to uphold an earlier government decision pronouncing his Holy Synod illegitimate and supporting the schismatic Synod of Met-

ropolitan Pimen (*Index* 3/1996, 5/1996). The Synod was ruled illegitimate because most of its members were appointed by the former Communist regime. (RFE/RL)

Two criminal cases are currently pending against **Yovka Atanassova**, editor of the daily paper *Starozagorsky Novini* in the town of Stara Zagora. In March Atanassova was given three consecutive sentences totalling eight months in prison, in connection with a series of articles on links between secret service informants and government officials. The pending cases are thought to relate to the same series of articles. (RSF)

BURMA

Thai journalists, in Rangoon to cover the official visit of their prime minister on 15 and 16 May, found their reports subject to restrictions and their movements closely monitored by the State Law and Order Council (SLORC). Reporters were issued with visas valid for only two days and barred from covering activities of National League for Democracy (NLD) leader Aung San Suu Kyi. (CPJ, *Bangkok Post*)

An NLD congress, planned to commemorate the anniversary of their annulled 1990 election victory, was suppressed on 27 May. Only 10 members of the NLD executive were allowed to meet at Suu Kyi's house, while NLD sources report that in the preceding week some 316 party members were detained in a

nationwide clampdown aimed at thwarting the gathering. In recent months roadblocks near her residence have prevented Suu Kyi's weekly rallies and she has been prohibited from speaking in public. (Reuters, SWB, *Independent, South China Morning Post*)

Five close associates of Suu Kyi, including her cousin **Cho Aung Than**, her photographer **Ko Sunny** and politician **Hon Myint**, were detained in late June and accused of smuggling her videotaped speeches out of the country. (Reuters)

BURUNDI

On 5 June security forces searched the house of the banned UPRONA party leader **Charles Mukasi**, allegedly looking for subversive documents, after he criticised recent searches of the homes of other UPRONA members. The mainly Tutsi party came under attack again at the end of the month when soldiers surrounded its headquarters on 25 June in a bid to prevent a meeting going ahead. (Agence France Presse, United Nations)

CAMEROON

The 5 May edition of the biweekly *L'Expression*, carrying an interview with the former health minister Titus Edzoa, was confiscated from kiosks in Yaounde by security forces. Another privately owned newspaper, *L'Anecdote*, which alleged that a meeting had taken place between opposition leader John Fru Ndi and

Edzoa, was also seized the following day. (RSF)

CANADA

The federal government announced in May that it would appeal a World Trade Organisation ruling against Canada's restriction on foreign advertising and publishing interests, particularly its tax on split-run magazine editions. Designed to protect Canada's domestic magazine publishing industry, the restrictions also place a per-centage limit on foreign ownership of publishing assets. (Reuters)

CHILE

On 9 June the leaders of the **Chilean Association of Relatives of Disappeared Prisoners** (AFDDC) received anonymous telephone death threats. The threats are thought to be connected to a confrontation two days earlier during which inhabitants of the Colonia Dignidad, a secretive German colony in southern Chile, used vehicles, water jets and loudspeakers to disrupt a demonstration by various human rights organisations. The association had recently denounced the disappearance of 103 Chileans who were taken to Dignidad during the dictatorship of General Pinochet. (Reuters, *Independent*, Equipo Nizkor)

CHINA

Bao Tong (*Index* 2/1995, 4/1996) was released after 11 months of house arrest on 26 April. His release is conditional on his moving away from central Beijing. He has been

deprived of his political rights for a year and forbidden to speak to journalists, mix with activists or publish. (AI)

China reacted angrily to the inclusion of **Zhang Yuan's** banned *East Palace, West Palace* (a co-production with France) in the Cannes Film Festival, confiscating the director's passport in early April and later prohibiting the **Zhang Yimou** (*Index* 6/1995) film *Keep Cool* from taking part in the competition. (*Variety*, Reuters)

Restrictions are to be placed on mainland tourists hoping to visit Hong Kong between 15 June and 15 July and all trips to the territory cancelled between 30 June and 2 July, it was announced in early May. In an effort to minimise disruption to the island and limit permit seekers planning to overstay, tours will be reduced from 22 to 14 a day and children under 18 banned from visiting Hong Kong during the handover. (*South China Morning Post*)

Journalists were ordered in late May to avoid seven 'forbidden zones' in their coverage of the handover of Hong Kong on 1 July. Reports on 'any incident...unfavourable to the transition' or on labour disputes in the territory and social problems on the mainland are prohibited, as are references to recent British policy in Hong Kong or to speeches by British officials. (*Daily Telegraph*)

Labour activists **Li Wenming** and **Guo Baosheng** were sentenced to three-and-a-half

years in prison on 29 May, six months after they first stood trial on charges of conspiring to subvert the government. After a lengthy detention period, they have been granted release dates of November and December 1997 respectively. (HRW)

Three hundred magazines and newspapers are to be closed down, it was announced in mid-May, in accordance with Communist Party announcements on the need to 'strengthen macro control over the journalistic industry'. Negative news is also to be reduced and reports on 'seamy aspects' of society restricted in order to safeguard social stability. (*Sing Tao Jih Pao*)

Shanghai dissident **Bao Ge** was released from detention on 4 June, serving a three-year sentence at a re-education-through-labour camp. (SWB)

Recent publications: *Prisoner List — 1989 Prisoners Eight Years On* (AI, May 1997, 31pp); *The Eighth Anniversary of the 1989 Massacre — Those Who Have Been Silenced* (AI, April 1997, 17pp)

COLOMBIA

Two human rights workers were killed in their home in Bogotá on 19 May. **Carlos Mario Calderón** and **Elsa Constanza Alvarado**, university professors who worked for the human rights body, the Centre for Research and Popular Education (CINEP), were shot dead by a group of masked gunmen who identified themselves as members of the attorney general's office.

● ●

LI WENMING

Statement to the court

Broadly speaking, my case is distinguished by the fact that it is directly con-cerned with the question of propagating political opinions. Yet my ideas and opinions never went beyond the stage of discussion. Moreover, the parameters of this discussion were always narrow and took place within the confines of a tiny apartment. Only a very small number of people were influenced by the discussion and it was conducted over a short period of time. Society suffered no harmful results, public order was definitely not threatened and the interests of the people were in no way harmed. I firmly believe that there is not one article in Chinese law that could confirm I have committed the crime of counter-revolution or of conspiring to subvert the government. Indeed, even using the evidence set out in the official indictment, it is still impossible to come to this conclusion. The case itself and the arguments on which the indictment is grounded are mutually contradictory. There are six clear points which negate the charges of counter-revolution:

1. We had no programme to oppose the government

2. We had no leaders

3. We had no real strength

4. We had no plan of action

5. We undertook no operations or activities

6. There were no serious results

I believe that the court officials will pay sufficient attention to all these six points. I also believe that history itself will make the final judgment — namely that to speak out is not a crime.

In connection with my case, I would also ask the court to take into consideration the following four points:

● ●

●●●

1. That the court pays close attention to the provisions in Chinese law and not casually label its own citizens with the crime of 'government subversion'. I hope that this crime is not just a modern-day version of the days when Chinese rulers could lock up anyone they chose.

2. That the court will implement the various articles and supplementary articles in the constitution that grant citizens the right of freedom to express opinions.

3. That our society doesn't strangle attempts at constructive criticism. Even if our views are wide and varied, even if our ideologies and outlooks differ in a thousand different ways, we are all still citizens of China, and no Chinese government has the right either to oppress the Chinese people or to falsely accuse them.

4. That people can become genuine masters of their own fate, that the tide of the great River Yangtze can continue to flow from west to east without obstruction and that democracy can take root and flower all over the vast Asian continent. It is not important whether this democracy is called socialist democracy or reform democracy, but only that it is genuine democracy with the people having genuine sovereign rights.

I believe that a civilised and dignified system of government should have the capacity to accommodate these ideas. A government that tolerates dissent is one that respects its own policies; and a government that acknowledges conscience is one that acknowledges history itself.

An edited excerpt from Li's speech, taken from China Labour Bulletin *no.34. China Labour Bulletin can be contacted on clb@hkstar.com*

●●

Elsa's father, Carlos Alvarado Pantoja, also died and her mother was severely injured. Her one-year-old son survived by hiding in a cupboard. (AI, Reuters, Derechos Human Rights)

CONGO (BRAZZAVILLE)

Radio France Internationale correspondent in Brazzaville, **Alain Shungu**, was denied a temporary visa to France on 20 June. Shungu and three members of his family were evacuated to Libreville after repeated attacks on their home. The Congo (Brazzaville) cabinet has criticised the radio station for its 'unbalanced' coverage of the crisis. (RSF)

COTE D'IVOIRE

Daniel Opeli, a reporter with the independent newspaper *La Voie*, was severely beaten by police while covering a meeting of the student organisation FESCI which took place at the University of d'Abobo-Adjame on 15 May. (CPJ)

CROATIA

The satirical weekly *Feral Tribune* was fined US$7,000 at the beginning of May for printing a 'pornographic' cover which featured a photomontage of the prominent eastern Slavonia politician, Tomislav Mercep, urinating. On 7 May it was announced that the magazine's editor, **Viktor Ivancic**, and a staff journalist, **Marinko Culic**, are to be retried on charges of insulting President Tudjman. They were acquitted of the charge in September 1996

(*Index* 4/1996, 6/1996). (RFE/RL)

On 19 May thieves broke into the **Beli Manastir TV** studio in eastern Slavonia and stole vital equipment, forcing the station off the air indefinitely. (SWB)

Zdravko Tomac, the Social Democratic candidate in the presidential elections, was denied permission to hold a rally in Zagreb's Jelacic Square on 13 June. President Franjo Tudjman held a rally in the square on 12 June and Liberal candidate Vladimir Gotovac spoke there the previous night. (RFE/RL)

CUBA

Attacks on the independent press continued throughout early summer. On 31 May **Joaquín Torres**, director of the independent news agency Habana Press, was attacked outside his house by four people believed to be working for the Department of State Security. On the same day, **Rafaela Lasalle**, director of the Agencia Oriental de Prensa, was threatened by members of the Vigilance and Protection Unit. Five days later police visited the mother of **Raul Rivero**, director of the independent agency Cuba Press, to tell her that her son would have to cease his activities as a journalist or leave the country. Press agency workers were also targeted: Agencia de Prensa Independiente correspondents **Mirtha Leyva** and **Jesus Zuniga** were interrogated on 14 and 18 June respectively while **Juan Carlos Cespedes** of Libre

Oriental was held for questioning for six days and pressed to reveal the source for recent reports he had filed. (AI, RSF)

New rules regulating the activities of foreign correspondents took effect in early June. Under the regulations, administered by the government-created International Press Centre, news correspondents are required to report 'with objectivity, sticking strictly to the facts' and local journalists are to be hired only through government offices. Removal of accreditation is threatened for those who do not comply. (IAPA)

Recent publications: *Dangerous Writers — Freedom of Expression in Cuba* (PEN, May 1997, 28pp)

CZECH REPUBLIC

Miroslav Sladek, leader of the far-right Republican Party, was cleared of libel by Prague's municipal court on 29 May. The case had been brought by the Romany Democratic Congress in connection with disparaging comments about Roma people which Sladek made in parliament in July 1996. In February Sladek was stripped of his parliamentary immunity and briefly arrested after he made a speech in which he said: 'We can only regret that we killed too few Germans' during World War II. (SWB, *International Herald Tribune*)

On 1 June new regulations came into force allowing Czech citizens to see any files

ILKAY ADALI

Living without fear

When distinguished Turkish-Cypriot journalist Kutlu Adali was shot dead outside his home in the Kizilbash district of Nicosia on 7 July 1996 (Index 5/1996), police in Turkish-occupied northern Cyprus said they would conduct a 'widespread investigation'. Nothing has been heard of this investigation since. The journalist's widow, Ilkay Adali, who was away at the time of the murder, has herself received threatening letters and phone calls. She remains sceptical of the Turkish authorities' intentions

'The only thing they keep on telling me is that I should not be talking to journalists. Why not? I have nothing to hide. I want people to know.

'When I found out what happened, I tried to get a ticket back with Cyprus Turkish Airways. I was told they were fully booked. I was unable to return until after the funeral. And without my knowledge our house had been searched — my husband's papers and all.

'I put a photograph of him and some flowers on the spot where he died. Within hours they had been removed, a bulldozer came and covered the street with asphalt. Now what should I make of that? I also offered my husband's books, 31,000 in all, to a public library to be opened in his memory. One year on and I am still waiting.

'One of the main suspects for my husband's killing, a Turkish-Cypriot shopkeeper and reserve officer, still wanders around armed and in military uniform. He called me at home to deny he was one of the murderers and warning that we should all be careful about what we say. He fears for his own life too.

'Fear is not always the best counsellor, that's what Kutlu Adali used to say. Living in fear means dying time and time again. You'll die anyway, that's true, but you can choose to die only once.'

Interviewed by Sergios Zambouras

kept on them by the StB, the former secret police. Names of any third parties mentioned in the files will be deleted before the documents are released. (SWB)

DEMOCRATIC REPUBLIC OF CONGO

Karen Lajon (*Index* 3/1997), a correspondent with the French weekly *Le Journal du Dimanche*, was again expelled from the country on 10 May, despite the fact that her visa was valid. Reuters journalists **John Chiahemen, Nicholas Kotch** and **William Wallis, Howard Burditt**, Reuters photographer, and **Robert Wiener** of Cable News Network (CNN) were also expelled for having allegedly 'covered the crisis in Zaire in a tendentious manner'. (RSF)

On 26 May state television announced that the newly formed government of the Democratic Republic of Congo (DRC) had banned all demonstrations and political party activity until further notice. Meanwhile, state controlled radio announced the banning of commercials on private stations to end 'disorder and anarchy'. (Voix du Congo, Congo Television, *Guardian*)

Soldiers broke up a march in Kinshasa on 29 May, shooting into the air and beating people with gun butts and batons, as several thousand supporters of opposition leader Etienne Tshisekedi protested against his exclusion from government and the presence of Rwandans in the army. (Reuters, *Guardian*)

DENMARK

Toeger Seidenfaden, editor of the daily paper *Politiken*, was given a 20-day suspended sentence in early May for having published the diary of an EU commissioner without her permission. He claimed he had her 'silent acquiescence' to publish — the commissioner concerned, Ritt Bjerregeard denies this. (*International Herald Tribune*)

EGYPT

Censors seized 50 books judged to contravene public morality or offend Islam, it was reported on 31 May. The seizures took place after recommendations to the censorship board by Al-Azhar Islamic Research Academy, the Sunni Islamic authority. Meanwhile, the Matarya court of appeal for misdemeanours upheld a ruling against author **Ala'a Hamid** (*Index* 4&5/1994), sentencing him to one year's imprisonment with hard labour, a fine of US$60 and the banning of his novel *Al-Firash* (The Bed). He was charged with producing and possessing printed materials of an indecent nature which encourage immorality. (*Middle East Times*)

Cairo University engineering professor, **Ahmad al-Ahwany**, was arrested on 24 April and ordered to be held for 15 days' administrative detention in Isteqbal Tora prison. He was arrested after a photocopy shop owner called the police after he saw the professor making copies of a bulletin titled *Al-Tadamun*

(Solidarity), which criticises the new agricultural law that gives landowners the right to evict tenants after a certain period. He was accused of preparing documents for distribution that would damage public interests and destabilise public order. On 17 June journalist **Hamdien Sabbahi**, director of the Al-Watan Al-Arabi Information Centre, and seven other members of the National Committee for the Defence of Farmers were arrested in a dawn raid by a State Security Investigation (SSI) force for opposition to the new law. Sabbahi was ordered to be detained for 15 days. (OMCT, *Middle East Times*, Centre for Human Rights Legal Aid)

Two actors — **Maali Zayed** and **Mamdouh Wafi** — successfully appealed against suspended sentences imposed in March and were acquitted on 18 May of any wrongdoing for appearing in the film *Abu Al-Dahab* (Father of Gold). **Samir Abdel Azim**, the producer of the film which tells the story of a drug trafficker, was ordered to pay US$1,500 after four scenes were judged by the court and the censors as offensive. (*Middle East Times*)

Gamal Abu Ali, a Jordanian-Canadian researcher for Human Rights Watch/Middle East, was denied entry to Egypt on arrival at Cairo airport on 20 June. He was held at the airport overnight and deported to Paris the next day. He had been due to join his colleague Joe Stork and discuss human rights in Egypt with various bodies, including the Ministry of Foreign

Affairs. (Centre for Human Rights Legal Aid)

Ibrahim Issa, editor-in-chief of *Al-Doustour* was charged with defamation on 24 June following a complaint by the minister of transport Suleimane Metualli. He is accused of publishing articles in March and April critical of ministers' wealth. (RSF)

ESTONIA

On 20 May the government approved a bill regulating the distribution of works containing pornography and promoting violence or cruelty. The bill envisages restricting access to such works for minors (defined as those under 18 years of age) and prohibiting pornography from display. The initial decision on what constitutes pornography or violence will rest with the importers and publishers themselves. Any traders who are in doubt about the content of a particular publication will be able to apply to a special commission, set up by the Ministry of Culture, for a ruling on what constitutes pornography or the promotion of violence. (SWB)

ETHIOPIA

Ato Assefa Maru, a member of the executive committee of the Ethiopian Human Rights Council (EHRCO), was shot dead on 8 May on his way to his office by police officers who claim they discovered him with accomplices preparing for an act of terrorism. Witnesses, however, have stated that Maru was assassinated. (EHRCO)

FRANCE

In late April an anti-racist group announced plans to sue the French far-right leader Jean-Marie Le Pen for his statement that gas chambers had nothing to do with anti-Semitism and were instead a 'detail' of World War II. Le Pen was fined for similar remarks in 1987. (Reuters, *International Herald Tribune*)

On 14 May **Gael Cornier**, a correspondent with the Associated Press (AP) news agency, was detained while taking photographs of the arrest of demonstrators at a rally in Saint-Denis. Cornier was assaulted by five policemen and his camera seized, while another correspondent who came to his rescue was also hit. While in detention Cornier was prevented from contacting his editors. He was released some hours later. (RSF)

Three-month custodial sentences passed on rap singers **Bruno Lopez** and **Didier Morville** of the group NTM (*Index* 1/1997) last November for insulting the police, were reduced on appeal on 23 June. They have been replaced by two-month suspended sentences and fines of US$4,300 each. (Reuters)

A bomb exploded at the offices of *Corse-Matin* on 23 June, causing some material damage. The daily was the subject of similar attacks in 1992 and 1994. (RSF)

GABON

Independent radio station *La Radio Commercial* in Libreville has been off the air since 20 May when its transmitter was completely destroyed in an act of vandalism by several unidentified armed men. (CPJ)

GERMANY

Angela Marquardt (*Index* 2/1997) went on trial on 6 June charged with maintaining an Internet site providing a link to the banned leftist magazine *Radikal*. The case has been delayed while witnesses are called. (Reuters, *International Herald Tribune*)

Habib Mokni, exiled journalist and editor of the quarterly *al-Insan*, was arrested on 19 June in transit at Frankfurt, apparently as a result of an extradition claim issued by the Tunisian government. He is likely to face imprisonment if returned to Tunisia. (PEN)

In late June legislation was introduced requiring Internet service providers to be licensed. The legislation, the first attempt in Europe to regulate the Internet, is expected to set a precedent for other western nations. (*Computing*)

GHANA

Accra-based US diplomat **Nicolas Robertson** was expelled on 22 May on the orders of the government after allegedly expressing concerns about local press laws and the criminal libel trials of the editors of the independent bi-weeklies the *Ghanaian Chronicle* and *The Free Press*. (West African Journalists' Association)

GUATEMALA

María Francisca Ventura and her family were subjected to repeated acts of intimidation by presumed members of the security forces in late April and early May. Ventura believes she is being targeted after giving testimony to an Amnesty International delegation in April about the death of her husband, Manuel Saquic Vásquez in July 1995. Saquic Vásquez was co-ordinator of a Kaqchikel Maya human rights committee in Panajabal and the sole witness to the abduction by security forces of another member of the committee. (AI)

Oscar Madrigal, director of the news programme *OIR*, was attacked outside his home on 31 May when two men and a women pulled up in a car and opened fire. He escaped uninjured. *OIR*, which is broadcast daily in Puerto Barrios on Radio Atlantida, had recently carried a series of reports about the neglect of the city's roads by the mayor's office. The attack is one of several made against Guatemalan journalists since the beginning of May. (CCPJ)

HONDURAS

On 12 May over 2,000 armed soldiers and police attacked thousands of indigenous and black protesters who had set up camp in front of the presidential palace in Tegucigalpa. The demonstrators were protesting the recent assassinations of two of their leaders and demanding land for the Chortis people of Ocotepeque and Copan provinces.

The attack took place five hours before an accord was scheduled to be signed by government and march leaders. Three people were injured, including a pregnant women and a child; food was destroyed and belongings looted. (Derechos Human Rights, Reuters)

HONG KONG

Students at the Hong Kong Polytechnic University were refused permission to hold a fund-raising event for Amnesty International in early May. The event, similar to one held on the campus last October, would have included a display of information on human rights. It was turned down as a 'political function' and on the grounds that outside groups are prohibited from raising funds on campus. (Reuters, *South China Morning Post*)

The Hong Kong branch of publishers Viking-Penguin have been accused of failing to publicise a collection of Wei Jingsheng's prison writings, *The Courage to Stand*, it was reported in late May. The book, until recently only stocked in the *South China Morning Post* bookshop, has apparently been seen as too sensitive to promote during the handover period. Meanwhile, bookshops in the Sino United group are refusing to stock politically problematic works, including the memoirs of defector Xu Jiatun and Li Zhisui's *Private Life of Chairman Mao*. (*Guardian*, MISA)

On 26 May Tung Chee-hwa, Hong Kong's new chief exec-

utive, told journalists at a meeting of the Hong Kong News Executive Association to 'shoulder social responsibility' in their reporting and exercise greater sensitivity when reporting on China's policy on territorial integrity. (*South China Morning Post*)

Legislation banning demonstrations and political groups that are deemed a threat to national security (*Index* 3/1997) was passed by the Provisional Legislature on 14 June. Protest rallies similar to the annual 4 June demonstration will still be tolerated, said Tung Chee-hwa, but must be more subdued. Under the new regulations the defacement of the Chinese flag, the display of protest symbols and the singing of chants critical of the mainland are also to be prohibited. (Reuters)

Recent publications: *Basic Rights at Risk — Comments on the HKSAR Consultation Documents of April 1997* (AI, April 1997, 17pp); *Prison Conditions in 1997* (HRW/Asia, June 1997, 51pp)

INDIA

In late April Mira Nair, the director of the film, *Kama Sutra*, announced her intention to sue censors in India for harassment and loss of revenue after they demanded further cuts to the film before it could be released. The Indian censorship board over-ruled an earlier order clearing the film after about a dozen scenes of explicit nudity were cut. They are now demanding further cuts. (*South China Morning Post, Guardian*)

The government approved a broadcasting bill to regulate electronic media on 5 May. Under the new law television and radio stations will be licensed by an autonomous body, the Broadcasting Authority of India, foreign investment in local stations will be limited to 49 per cent and cross-media ownership restricted to 20 per cent. (*Asia Times*)

Lawyer **T Puroshotham** of the Andhra Pradesh Civil Liberties Committee was attacked while walking home on 27 May. Human rights workers in the area believe the assault was the work of a government-backed group set up to counter their activities. (AI)

Arundhati Roy is to be charged with obscenity over scenes in her debut novel *The God of Small Things*, it was announced on 18 June. The charge is to be brought under public interest litigation in her home state of Kerala. (*South China Morning Post, Sydney Herald*)

INDONESIA

Thirteen members of the banned People's Democratic Party, including the leader **Budiman Sudjatmiko** (*Index* 5/1996, 2/1997), were found guilty of subversion on 28 April. Sentences ranged from 18 months to 13 years, with the harshest passed on Sudjatmiko. (*Guardian*)

On 4 May **Sri Bintang Pamungkas** (*Index* 3/1997) began a 34-month gaol term after the Supreme Court upheld his sentence for

defaming the president during a speech he gave in Germany in April 1995. Eight days later he was dismissed from his post as a lecturer at the University of Indonesia. (*Jakarta Post*)

Banners and posters depicting political leaders were banned from public display during Indonesia's month-long general election campaign. Slogans and chants supporting an informal alliance between ousted Indonesian Democratic Party leader Megawati Sukarnoputri and the United Development Party (PPP) were also prohibited and several Jakarta-based editors reported receiving phone calls from the military office asking them not to run a statement issued by Megawati on 22 May. Meanwhile, a PPP-owned publication, *Buletin Suara Bintang*, was branded as illegal on 20 May. Its publisher, journalist **Anding Sukiman**, is reported to be under police investigation. Other magazines affected by the election concerns included the normally outspoken *D&R*, which pulped 15,000 copies of its election issue and replaced them with an edition taking a 'milder' approach to allegations of election fraud. (Reuters, Institute for the Studies on Free Flow of Information)

Over 250 people are believed to have been killed in political rioting during the campaign period, the most violent in President Suharto's 31 years of rule. In addition, the Alliance of Independent Journalists reports that more than 20 journalists were beaten and harassed, many losing camera

equipment and film, while covering the campaign in Jakarta and Surabaya. (*Guardian*, Institute for the Studies on Free Flow of Information)

The Independent Election Monitoring Committee (KIPP) reported systematic violations of election rules during polling on 29 May. Electoral irregularities included multiple voting, intimidation of party witnesses and discrimination in the treatment of voters. KIPP also criticised the ruling Golkar party for restricting access to the election database, rendering any independent check impossible. Meanwhile, the National Commission on Human Rights has accused Golkar-affiliated organisations of providing food and drink in areas of low Golkar support in a bid to win votes. (Reuters, *Asia Intelligence Wire*)

In early June General Hartono, the newly appointed information minister, warned journalists 'not to make news which will push the government to revoke the publishing licence'. Meanwhile one senior editor has reportedly been dismissed, two sent on enforced leave and another demoted as a consequence of government displeasure over reports on vote-rigging during the elections. (*South China Morning Post*)

On 18 June the Ministry of Tourism, Posts and Telecommunications announced plans to control Internet access. 'Pornography [and] things that hamper or threaten national security' will be controlled and 'the values of the nation' applied. (RSF)

Mohammad Sayuti, an investigative journalist on the Sulawesi paper *Pos Makasar*, died on 12 June after a violent beating. His death has been linked with his recent reports on local corruption. (Institute for the Studies on Free Flow of Information)

Recent publication: *Freedom of Expression and the 1997 Elections* (A19, May 1997, 33pp)

IRAN

The 23 May elections were criticised for their undemocratic nature. Only four of the 238 candidates for the presidency passed the stringent selection procedures of the ruling clergy, the Council of Guardians, while no women, Sunni or Bahai Muslims, Christians, Jews or Zoroastrians were permitted to stand. Restrictions on the media continued with the daily *Hamshahri*, a pro-Rafsanjani paper, accused of bias by the elections campaign commission for publishing a supplement promoting Mohammad Khatami. Meanwhile the Tehran newspaper *Salam*, which also supported Khatami's candidacy, succumbed to official pressure and stopped reporting on the election altogether after 5 May. (*About Iran*, HRW)

Faraj Sarkoohi (*Index* 6/1996, 1/1997, 2/1997, 3/1997) went to trial on 24 June on charges of spying and attempting to leave Iran illegally. In spite of reassurances by the judiciary, Sarkoohi has

not been allowed a lawyer and the trial is in camera. (RSF)

Recent publications: *Human Rights Violations against Shi'a Religious Leaders and their followers* (AI, June 1997, 27pp); *Eight Years of Death Threats to Salman Rushdie* (AI, May 1997, 5pp); *Leaving Human Rights Behind — The Context of the Presidential Elections* (HRW/Middle East, May 1997, 10pp)

IRAQ

Bekir Dogan, correspondent for Kurdish MED-TV, disappeared on 16 May following an attack by Turkish and Kurdistan Democratic Party (KDP) forces on Kurdish institutions in northern Iraq. Dogan was reporting on the fighting in the north following the Turkish invasion on 14 May. (MED-TV)

ISRAEL

Schools in East Jerusalem were ordered by the Ministerial Committee on Jerusalem Affairs in June to replace the Jordanian curriculum with the curriculum used by Arab schools inside Israel. A decision that Israeli rather than Palestinian school inspectors administer Palestinian *tawjihi*, or high school exams, in East Jerusalem was rescinded after protests. The committee also decided to block PNA attempts to run the schools. (*Guardian*, *Jerusalem Times*)

Legislation that will ban the publication and distribution of literature intended to induce religious conversion passed its first reading in the

Knesset in May. The bill's sponsors — Moshe Gafni of the ultra-Orthodox United Torah Judaism Party and Nissim Zvili of the Labour Party — claim that they hope to counter Christian missionary organised campaigns. Zvili said that the bill was not intended to hinder Christian worship or personal possession of Christian literature. (*The Times*)

JAPAN

Miyagi prefecture have banned an elementary school history textbook, it was reported in early May. The book, widely used in the area and authored by local teachers, was condemned as deviating from Education Ministry guidelines in its presentation of the Nanking Massacre and the Sino-Japanese war. (*Mainichi Daily News*)

JORDAN

The 1993 Press and Publications Law was drastically amended by royal decree on 17 May to impose sweeping restrictions on the press. The changes include an amended Article 40 that now bans the publication of any information that 'offends the King or the Royal Family', 'damages national unity', 'foments hatred' or 'insults heads of state of Arab, Islamic or friendly countries'. Publication of 'false news or rumours that offend public interests or state departments' is also prohibited. Violation of the regulations can lead to suspension or closure of publications with publication resuming only at the discretion of the information minister. Other new changes include a drastic increase in the capital that must be invested in publications — a move seen as threatening to smaller weeklies that have been highly critical of the government — and a requirement that all chief editors must have 10 years' experience as journalists. On 20 May during a demonstration in Amman against the press law amendments police attempted to confiscate cameras and 10 journalists were arrested. (CPJ, Reuters)

Recent publication: *A Death Knell for Free Expression? The New Amendments to the Press and Publications Law* (HRW/Middle East, June 1997, 15pp)

KAZAKHSTAN

Mukhtar Ismailov, director of the Association of Independent Electronic Mass Media of Central Asia and Kazakhstan, complained on 2 May that independent radio and television in the area had 'practically ceased to exist'. Since the government commission for allocating radio and TV frequencies was set up at the end of 1996 (*Index* 1/1997, 3/1997), 27 independent regional radio and television stations have been closed down by the Kazakh authorities. (SWB)

KENYA

Jacob Otieno and **Jacob Waweru**, photojournalists for the daily *East African Standard*, were assaulted and injured by police on 29 May while covering a rally for constitutional

reforms at Uhuru Park in Nairobi. The following day paramilitary troops and riot police broke up another reform rally in Uhuru Park with tear gas and batons, beating opposition members, journalists and bystanders. In response to the disturbances, President Moi published the Peaceful Assemblies Bill which will require convenors of processions and political meetings to obtain prior permission from the district officer. (*Guardian*, Reuters, RSF, NDIMA, United Nations)

Dissident politician **Sheikh Khalid Balala** was refused entry to the country on 6 June and returned to Germany. Leading opposition members Raila Odinga, Kenneth Matiba and Ngengi Muigai were beaten up by security officers as they protested Balala's expulsion. (Reuters)

The government turned down a request by **George Nthenge** MP on 12 June to appoint a committee to review the cases of more than 30 banned publications, arguing that the sedition or immoral grounds on which they had been banned had not changed. (NDIMA)

Recent publication: *Juvenile Injustice — Police Abuse and Detention of Street Children in Kenya* (HRW/Africa, June 1997, 155pp)

KYRGYZSTAN

Sentences passed on *Res Publica* journalists in late May (*Index* 5/1996, 2/1997, 3/1997) were reduced by a

municipal court on 10 June. Editor-in-chief **Zamira Sydykova**'s 18-month sentence was reduced to one year in a penal colony while **Aleksandr Alyanchikov**'s sentence was changed from 18 months to a one-year suspended sentence. The decision to bar **Bektash Shamshiev** and **Marina Sivasheva** from journalism for 18 months was also overturned. (RFE/RL)

LEBANON

Recent publications: *Antoinette Chahin — Torture and Unfair Trial* (AI, June 1997, 7pp); *An Alliance Beyond the Law — Enforced Disappearances in Lebanon* (HRW/Middle East, May 1997, 36pp); *Restrictions on Broadcasting* (HRW/Middle East, April 1997, 21pp)

MACEDONIA

The Interior Ministry brought charges against the mayors and other officials of the predominantly Albanian towns of Gostivar and Tetovo on 5 May for ordering the Albanian flag to be flown from public buildings on state holidays. In other areas the Turkish flag was also raised, in violation of a law barring the display of foreign symbols. On 26 May police broke up armed clashes between Macedonians and ethnic Albanians and Turks protesting the charges. In a bid to defuse the growing crisis, the government drafted a new law that would give Albanian and Turkish minorities the right to fly the flags of Albania or Turkey at private, cultural, or sporting events. They may also display their flags on state holidays if they also fly the Macedonian banner. They will not be allowed to fly their flags from public buildings, however. (RFE/RL)

MALAYSIA

On 29 April opposition MP **Lim Guang Eng** was found guilty of sedition and spreading false news after publishing a pamphlet which criticised the judiciary's actions in a 1994 rape case. He was fined US$6,000 by the high court and faces disqualification from his seat and a ban from politics for the next five years. (*Asiaweek, Far Eastern Economic Review*)

In early May the Malaysian Indian Congress called for the censoring of scenes of violence, horror and sex in imported Tamil and Hindi films. The films have been blamed by community leaders for the 'moral degradation' of Indian youth in Malaysia. (*Straits Times*)

Twenty-four people have been arrested on obscenity charges and 2,393 pornographic videos and CDs seized this year, it was reported in mid-May. Those charged face a gaol term of between six months and three years or a heavy fine. (*Asia Intelligence Wire*)

Concerts by pop band The Zurah II and the rap group KRU have been banned by the state governments of Kedah, Perlis and Selangor because of potential 'negative effects' on youth, it was reported in early June. (*Straits Times*)

MAURITANIA

The 22 April edition of the independent weekly *La Tribune* was seized, apparently because of a report on drugs and an article about the former president. The 26 April edition of the weekly *Mauritanie Nouvelles* was also seized by the Interior Ministry and banned for a month. No official reasons were given for the seizures. (RSF)

MEXICO

On 7 May, **Gerardo González**, chairman of the Co-ordination of Non-Governmental Organisations for Peace (CONPAZ), received a series of anonymous death threats by phone. The calls came a few minutes after a radio programme read out a statement by CONPAZ denouncing the expulsion of international human rights monitors. González believes that the caller is the same person who threatened him by phone on several occasions during November 1996. (AI)

The offices of the **Human Rights Centre Miguel Agustin Pro Juarez** (PRODH) have been under surveillance by 20 unidentified armed men, believed to be members of the security forces, since 5 May. PRODH members have been followed, photographed and filmed in their daily activities and everyone entering the offices has been conspicuously registered. PRODH, which has been the target of intimidation and death threats before, believes that the present action is part of an orchestrated campaign of harassment against the organisation. (AI)

The body of **Jesus Bueno León**, director of the newspaper *Siete Dias*, was found on 22 May near the Chilpancingo-Tixtla highway in the state of Guerrero. He had been shot in the head and had a fractured spine. Two months previously León had expressed fears for his own safety because of 'certain arguments with high-ranking government officials and even co-workers' at *Siete Dias*. León's murder was followed by that of **Leonicio Pintor Garcia**, correspondent for the Chilpancingo newspaper *El Sol*, who was found dead on 2 June in the Ajolotero river in Guerrero state. The body showed signs of torture. (*MEXpress, Guardian*, IAPA, Reuters)

During the last week of May, 11 members of the opposition **Democratic Revolutionary Party** (PRD), were arrested or 'disappeared' in the Montaña region of Guerrero. Five others are being sought by the security forces while seven were detained on 25 May and held incommunicado for two days on charges of conspiracy and sedition. Four more PRD members were taken from their homes on 26 and 27 May and their current whereabouts are still unknown. (AI)

MICRONESIA

Sacked editor of FSM News, **Cherie O'Sullivan** (*Index* 3/1997), was refused re-entry into the country on 11 June when she tried to board a flight for Pohnpei after a brief business trip to Guam. The immigration department had previously asked O'Sullivan to 'regularise her immigration status'. (SWB, CPJ)

MONGOLIA

In mid-May **G Akim**, editor-in-chief of *Il Tovchoo*, reported that the KGB had accused him of divulging state secrets. Akim, who was interrogated on 16 April, had published details of a KGB intelligence-gathering operation targeting political parties and candidates and civic organisations. He now faces a court case and up to three years' imprisonment. (SWB)

MOZAMBIQUE

On 27 May President Joaquim Chissano ordered the opposition party **Renamo** to hand over all its military communications equipment on the grounds that it is interfering with the work of the state and other bodies. Renamo leader Afonso Dhlakama, however, is demanding the return of equipment brokered between him and the president until a time when it can be replaced by radios designed for civilian use. (SWB)

NAMIBIA

A draft Namibian Film Commission bill released on 24 May proposes that any film producer or film production company wishing to produce 'any type of film in Namibia' cannot do so without a valid film production license. The penalty for not complying with the regulations will be a fine of US$440 and/or six

months' imprisonment. (MISA)

The ruling party SWAPO reportedly imposed a news blackout on debates, including on national constitutional issues, at its second congress held from 28 May to 1 June. President Sam Nujoma opened the congress with renewed attacks against journalists (*Index* 2/1997). (MISA)

NIGER

Recent publication: *Harassment of Government Opponents Has Become Systematic* (AI, May 1997, 11pp)

NIGERIA

A government decree banning trade unions from affiliating with international labour bodies or trade secretariats without seeking the express permission of the government was put into effect in early May. (*West Africa*)

Three journalists released from detention in May have had conditions attached to their bail. **Ladi Olorunyomi**, a freelance journalist held incommunicado since 20 March (*Index* 3/1997), **Godwin Agbroko**, editor-in-chief of the privately owned magazine *The Week* and **George Onah**, defence correspondent for the independent newspaper *Vanguard,* were released without charge on 6, 7 and 14 May respectively. Their passports have been impounded and they have been forbidden to write about conditions in detention centres. Each is also required to report to military headquarters twice a week

until further notice. Agbroko had been held for five months while Onah had been in detention since 15 May 1996. (CPJ, PEN)

Olatunji Dare, former chair of the editorial board of the *Guardian* newspaper, was detained on 4 June at Lagos airport as he arrived back from the USA. He was released later the same day but his passport was retained by security agents. (Independent Journalism Centre)

A police statement issued in the federal capital Abuja on 11 June banned demonstrations by any group to mark the fourth anniversary of the annulled presidential election on 12 June 1993. (Reuters)

PAKISTAN

Copies of the English-language daily *Dawn* (*Index* 1/1997) were seized and burned by workers from the ruling Pakistan Muslim League (PML) as they were being distributed in Sukkur and Thatta on 6 and 7 May. Reports in *Dawn* claim the PML were retaliating against their report of a press conference given by Imdadullah Unnar, a former special assistant to the caretaker chief minister, in which he criticised the current chief minister of Sind Liaquat, Ali Khan Jatoi. Ali Khan Jatoi has issued a press release condoning the action and ordering an inquiry. (Pakistan Press Foundation)

Journalist **Shamsuddin Haider**, a producer for the state-run station Radio Pak-

● ●

DAOUD KUTTAB

Oh for a pen

I spent my first night being promised any minute that the release order would come and finally I realised that it wouldn't. The following day a young man from Gaza was posted to guard me at the office I was staying in. He had been demoted and transferred to Ramallah after hitting a fellow officer and was very angry with the world. I wanted a pen. Thinking that I would soon be released, I decided to use my time wisely by writing up a few contracts for people we'd just hired for the TV station. No way, said Mohammed, my host. At 11am the police chief called me in to his office and I met a US consular representative who wanted information about how I was being treated and so on. My eyes zoomed in on the pen in her hand and I asked her for it, and then I asked if I could have the pad. By the time the interview was over I was back with Mohammed, but this time with a pen and a pad given to me in front of the police chief. Now I could sit down and write up those stupid contracts.

As my visitation period was extending infinitely, I started reading the books that my family and another US official had brought me. One was the biography of Bloomburg and the other was a Le Carré spy novel. The only person to show interest in what I was reading was the person working the computer and typing the daily report which had to be faxed to Gaza police headquarters. He was from the Hebron area and was clearly the most educated of the police officers. I helped him with some tricks to improve his efficiency in using the computer and showed him how the spell-check works in Arabic. The rest of the time I kept on reading, while police officer after police officer came and went in the computer room where I was being 'held'. Finally one of them came up to me and said: 'Aren't you tired and bored of reading?' Surprised, I answered him that I read because I was bored. Thinking that this was an unusual question, I ignored it. During the seven days of my detention in two locations no less than five police officers asked me that same question, and of course I gave them the same answer.

During the long night-time hours, when I actually was tired of reading, I would talk to the officers. One detective — a husky young man from Gaza who loved sport — talked to me about his work. He was angry with journalists because, he said, they ruined his work by publishing stories before his investigations were complete and because they often got the story wrong. He told me about two recent deaths in which the local press rushed to declare the victims to

● ●

● ●

be land-dealers and their deaths homicides when they were neither, and how the police station was swamped with the families demanding an apology from the police. We also spoke about other issues and the subject of stolen Israeli cars was discussed. He naturally reminded me that this was big business for Israelis, with everyone, from insurance companies to the owners of the cars, benefiting. He said that he and his boys could easily stop the cars being brought in to the Ramallah area, but he turned to me and asked: 'But why should I do it?' In the end the recaptured cars would just end up with high-ranking police officers, some of whom already have late model cars, perhaps more than one — all stolen.

Late Saturday night I was transferred out of the police station to the Ramallah prison, apparently because the station was unable to deal with the steadily increasing number of journalists wanting to find out about me. When I arrived they had emptied a small room about three metres by four with a small window at waist level. I was shown the plastic mattress sponge block that acts as pillow and blanket, and then they locked the heavy door on me. It was late so I slept, and in the morning I woke up with faces popping in the tiny window and looking and me and then going and then others coming as if I was some monkey in a zoo. Later things eased off and some of the prisoners tried to talk to me saying that my story was all over the world and that I would soon be released. One man came to my room. He'd been imprisoned for murder during the Israeli rule and was now awaiting trial in a Palestinian court. He was also the prison chef and therefore he had some freedom of movement. Apparently someone told him I was a journalist so he came to me with a request. His friend, a police officer, was in jail for beating up a fellow officer and needed help. He wanted to be transferred to a jail in Gaza so that it would be easier for his family to see him. Could I help him write a letter to President Arafat asking to be transferred? Well, I needed to make some friends in my new gaol so I agreed. 'And by the way, please fill the letter with flowery language and words of praise for the president so that he will agree to the transfer,' he said. Having agreed to the request I had no choice, so I drafted a letter to: HIS EXCELLENCY PRESIDENT YASSER ARAFAT MAY GOD PROTECT HIM and ended it wishing for AN INDEPENDENT PALESTINIAN STATE UNDER THE LEADERSHIP OF THE GREAT LEADER, OUR SYMBOL, YASSER ARAFAT.

● ●

istan, was killed by two gunmen at his home in the southern Punjab town of Bahawalpur on 9 June. Haider had been receiving threatening telephone calls following programmes broadcast by the station during the Shi'ite commemorative festival in May. He is the second journalist to be killed in Pakistan this year (*Index* 2/1997). (RSF)

Manzar Imkani, the senior sub-editor of the daily newspaper *Jang*, was shot dead by unidentified men in his house in Karachi on the evening of 17 June. Imkani was an active volunteer for the human rights organisation the Ansar Burney Welfare Trust International. A week earlier **Mohammed Zeeshan**, another Trust employee, was attacked and brutally killed near his house in Karachi on 9 June on his way home from the Trust's office. (Human Rights News International)

Recent publication: *Time to Take Human Rights Seriously* (AI, June 1997, 43pp)

Daoud Kuttab (see page 120), prominent journalist and 1996 winner of the CPJ's International Press Freedom Award, was summoned from his home in East Jerusalem to the Palestinian police headquarters in Ramallah on 20 May and held without charge for seven days. His detention apparently stems from his live broadcasts of Palestinian Legislative Council proceedings which he produces through Al Quds University's educational television channel. Kuttab's arrest came after he was quoted in interviews with the *International Herald Tribune* and the *Washington Post* accusing the Palestinian Broadcasting Corporation of jamming his broadcasts in order to censor the Legislative Council's criticisms of Arafat's administration. US consular officials who visited him were told that Kuttab's detention was ordered personally by Yasser Arafat. (CPJ, *Jerusalem Times*)

On 30 May **Ayyub Uthman**, a lecturer at the Azhar University of Gaza, was arrested by police in connection with an article entitled 'Not For Reading Only' which he contributed to the weekly *Al Bihad* on a recent PNA report on financial mismanagement. (SWB)

Prime Minister Julius Chan urged voters in mid-June not to let the Sandline mercenaries crisis cloud their thinking. A nationwide liquor ban and night curfew have been declared to prevent election violence. An independent MP was killed and the president's helicopter attacked in the run-up to polling on 14 June. (SWB)

A fierce campaign has been launched against **Baruch Ivcher**, owner of **Canal 2 TV**, in connection with their broadcast of allegations of Leonor La Rosa's torture by fellow army intelligence agents (*Index* 3/1997). On 24 May the joint command of Peru's armed forces issued a press release accusing Ivcher of fomenting a news-media campaign aimed at 'harming the prestige and image of the armed forces'. A magazine close to the high command, *Gente*, also accused Ivcher of selling arms to Ecuador. Ivcher has taken refuge in Miami in order to escape a military warrant for his arrest. Meanwhile a law has been rushed through which enables the authorities to cancel the nationality of any naturalised citizen who defames the armed forces. (*Guardian*, Instituto Prensa y Sociedad, *Latin American Newsletters*)

The television programme **En Persona** was the subject of an official complaint by congressman Andres Reggiardo, on 27 May. The programme, directed by César Hildebrandt, had made public a document signed by Reggiardo about the establishment of a national network of governors, prefects and subprefects whose aim was to guarantee the re-election of President Fujimori. Reggiardo acknowledges the signature as his but claims that the contents of the document were false. Hildebrandt, who faces two lawsuits resulting from reports broadcast on *En Persona*, has since reported receiving threats over the controversial interview he broadcast with Leonor La Rosa. (Instituto Prensa y Sociedad)

On 29 May congress voted to remove three constitutional court judges after they ruled in January that Fujimori should not be allowed to run for a third term in 2000. This move coincides with the publication of a report by the InterAmerican Commission on Human Rights of the Organisation of American States (OAS) that highlights Peru's failure to separate the three branches of government. (Instituto Prensa y Sociedad)

On 3 June the offices of **America Television** were evacuated following a bomb scare. The station is known for its criticism of the Fujimori administration and its political affairs programme, *Revista Dominical*, recently carried a series of critical reports about official corruption and members of the armed forces. (Instituto Prensa y Sociedad)

One-hundred-and-fourteen prisoners gaoled for alleged terrorist activity by Peru's 'faceless' courts were released on 25 June as part of Fujimori's judicial review. Two hundred others are expected to be freed in the coming months. (Reuters)

PHILIPPINES

Danny Hernández, a columnist and news editor on the daily *People's Journal Tonight*, was shot dead as he left work in the early hours of 3 June. Hernández, who specialised in reporting on drug syndicates and cases of police corruption, is the third Philippine journalist to be murdered in 15 months. (IPI)

POLAND

At an open-air service on 29 May Cardinal Jozef Glemp

launched a fierce attack on the Education Ministry for publishing sex education textbooks with 'pornographic overtones'. He also criticised the government for attempting to remove religious instruction from kindergartens. (RFE/RL)

President Kwasniewski signed the new lustration law on 18 June and announced that, under its provisions, senior government officials will have to disclose any links they had with the country's former secret police. (RFE/RL)

ROMANIA

On 18 May the government amended the Education Act to allow minorities to be educated in their mother tongue. The decision overturned provisions in the 1995 law that banned vocational training and the establishment of new college and university faculties for minority-language students, in particular ethnic Hungarians. The amendments are still to be approved by parliament. (SWB)

RUSSIAN FEDERATION

Russia: Shareholders in *Komsomolskaya Pravda* voted in early May to replace the newspaper's chief editor, **Valery Simonov**, with Vladimir Sungorkin, an ex-chairman of the paper's board. Simonov and Sungorkin clashed in March over Sungorkin's proposal to sell a 20 per cent stake in the paper to Oneksimbank rather than the gas monopoly Gazprom. Simonov had argued that this move would lead to a loss of

independence for the paper. (RFE/RL)

Journalists in Nizhny Novgorod complained in early May of increasing pressure from local politicians to print only news favourable to the city administration in the run-up to the June gubernatorial elections. (RFE/RL)

Journalist **Yulia Olshanskaya** and her **Channel 2x2** cameraman **Valery Ivanov** were attacked by Liberal-Democratic Party leader Vladimir Zhirinovsky when they tried to film him being denied entry to the Victory Day ceremonies at the Tomb of the Unknown Soldier on 8 May. (CPJ)

Human rights activist **Oleg Pazyura** was arrested in Murmansk on 26 May and charged with slander and threatening behaviour towards an official. (AI)

On 4 June the State Duma adopted a resolution to 'strengthen state monitoring of the activities of **Russian Public TV** (ORT)' (*Index* 6/1996, 3/1997). According to the resolution, the network's financial position, use of federal property and compliance with tax laws will come under investigation. ORT has recently been criticised by the Duma for its unfavourable coverage of parliament. (RFE/RL)

Charges against **Valeriya Novodvorskaya** (*Index* 3/1996, 6/1996), leader of the Democratic Union, were dropped in early June. Novodvorskaya was accused of inciting racial hatred in two newspaper articles and on Estonian television in 1993 and 1994. (RFE/RL)

Laws were passed by the State Duma on 23 June severely curtailing the religious freedoms of all but the four religions considered 'traditional' in Russia — Orthodox Christianity, Islam, Judaism and Buddhism. Under the new regulations missionary work will be restricted and churches introduced into the country less than 15 years ago will be prohibited from possessing property. (SWB)

Chechnya: **NTV** war correspondent **Yelena Masyuk**, her cameraman **Ilya Mordyukov**, and sound technician **Dmitry Olchev** were abducted by six armed men in Achkhoi-Martan, western Chechnya on 10 May. A month later two reporters from the television production company **VID**, including **Ilyas Bogatyrev**, were kidnapped in Grozny. Six journalists, however, have been released. Local Urals journalists **Aleksandr Utrobin** and **Olga Bagautdinova** were released by Chechen security forces on 6 May, while **Yuri Arkhipov**, **Nikolai Mamulashvili** and **Lev Zeltser** of **Radio Russia** and **Nikolai Zagnoiko** of the **ITAR-TASS** agency (*Index* 3/1997) were set free on 6 June, apparently without ransom. (CPJ)

Tatarstan: **Aleksandr Postnov**, Kazan correspondent for *Ekpress-Khronika,* reported receiving several threatening phone calls on 11 June in connection with his recent investigations into Russian

involvement in arms shipments to the Rabani regime in Afghanistan. (CPJ)

RWANDA

Appolos Hakizimana, editor-in-chief of the independent bi-monthly *Umuravumba* and former editor of the weekly *Intego*, was shot dead by two unidentified people as he returned home in the capital Kigali on 27 April. Three weeks earlier, Hakizimana had been the target of an attempted kidnapping which was foiled by the intervention of his neighbours. (RSF, AI)

Amiel Nkuriza, editor-in-chief of the bi-weekly *Le Partisan* and *Intego,* was arrested without charge on 13 May, reportedly accused of inciting ethnic tension through the newspapers. The two issues of *Le Partisan* before his arrest were seized at the printing press. (AI)

SAUDI ARABIA

On 15 June the Saudi Embassy in London announced that journalists will not be permitted to attend the trial of two British nurses facing a possible death sentence over the alleged murder of a colleague in Saudi Arabia. (Reuters)

SENEGAL

On 4 June the appeal court upheld a decision by the magistrate's court last year to fine the privately owned Senegalese media company **Sud Communication** US$1 million for public defamation of a sugar-importing company.

Sud Communication is to appeal to a higher court. Nine days later **Abdoulaye Ndiaga Sylla**, vice-president of the group and director of *Sud Quotidien*, was charged along with two of the paper's reporters with defaming the head of state and spreading false news. (CPJ)

SERBIA-MONTENEGRO

Serbia: On 4 June Zeljko Raznatovic, better known as Arkan, threatened to sue **Cable News Network** (CNN) in connection with its documentary 'Wanted', which presented alleged evidence of Arkan's participation in war crimes in Croatia and Bosnia and described his close links to President Milosevic. CNN said it stands by its story. (RFE/RL)

Fininvest, the company that publishes the independent paper *Nasa Borba*, was given three days to pay US$78,000 in taxes on 11 June, following an inspection by the tax authorities. Earlier this year, Fininvest was ordered to pay US$130,000 in sales and other taxes. *Nasa Borba* has had six visits from tax officials in the past 36 months, none of which has found any serious financial irregularities. (FIEJ)

Federal Yugoslav information minister Goran Matic told the Serbian Journalists' Association annual congress on 14 June that the government plans to eliminate the distinction between dependent and independent media. 'All media are dependent,' he said, 'it is just a question of whom they are dependent on.' He continued:

'All journalists accredited with the federal government are equal and we will try to make that equality a reality, provided they are fair.' The Serbian information minister, Radmila Lientijevic, told the congress that the authorities plan to take measures against 480 pirate radio and TV stations and that they will introduce 'broadcasting discipline, in spite of foreign pressure'. (SWB)

Kosovo: Miladin Ivanovic, Socialist Party of Serbia (SPS) leader in the city of Pec, closed the studios of the independent radio station **BKTV** on 8 May. He said the station should not continue to broadcast news. (SWB, CPJ)

Police stopped a team of journalists from the paper *Bujku* as they returned from Prizren on 11 June. **Behlu Jashari, Ilaz Bylykbashi** and **Faik Binca** were interrogated about their trip and had their film confiscated. (*Kosova Communication*)

SIERRA LEONE

All political activity has been banned by the junta of Sierra Leone Armed Forces Revolutionary Council (AFRC) which seized power on 25 May in a coup led by Major Johnny Paul Koromah. (*Guardian*)

Freelance journalist **Ishmael Jalloh** was killed on 3 June as he covered fighting in Allentown between AFRC soldiers and Nigerian ECOMOG soldiers. (CPJ)

Phillip Neville, managing editor of the *Standard Times*

newspaper, went into hiding after he was assaulted on 4 June by two armed men who broke into his home on the pretext that he was harbouring a government minister. (CPJ)

During the week of 9 June, **Ojukutu Macaulay**, host of the on-air talk show *Good Morning Freetown* on **Sky FM**, went into hiding after being threatened by a group of AFRC soldiers for arguing against the recent coup. **Sylvester Rogers**, a stringer with the BBC, has also reportedly gone into hiding after learning that AFRC soldiers were trying to locate him. (CPJ)

Following a story in the independent *For di People* on 11 June about an AFRC delegation travelling to Libya to seek military backing, journalists were warned in mid-June to seek clarification through council headquarters before publishing sensitive security issues. (CPJ, *Financial Times*)

SINGAPORE

On 12 May **Tan Sek Min** was fined US$26,000 for possession of 36 videos or CD-ROMs classified as obscene by the board of film censors. (*Straits Times*)

Under new guidelines issued by the Singapore Broadcasting Authority in mid-May, the dialogue in television sitcoms and series is to be kept as free from English and local dialects as possible. (*Straits Times*)

On 29 May **Tang Liang Hong** (*Index* 2/1997, 3/1997) was ordered to pay damages of

US$5.8 million to members of the People Action's Party, including Prime Minister Goh Chok Hong, who had brought a series of defamation suits against him. (*Guardian*)

SLOVAKIA

The national referendum on membership of NATO and on procedures for electing the president was scrapped on 26 May after the prime minister, Vladimir Meciar, attempted to delete one of the questions from the ballot papers. The independent referendum commission announced a nine per cent turnout, after a massive boycott in protest at Meciar's move, and declared the vote invalid. Meciar opposed the question on whether the president should be elected directly or by parliament because it would have threatened his chance of assuming the presidency when Michal Kovac steps down next year. (*Guardian*)

The Bratislava offices of SITA, the country's first private news agency, were broken into and equipment stolen on 7 June, eight days before it was due to begin operating. The agency, which focuses on economic and political news, was set up in direct competition with the state-run Slovak press agency, TASR. (RFE/RL)

SOUTH AFRICA

Amena Frense, the current affairs and news editor on SABC's programme, *Good Morning South Africa*, was prohibited from commenting to the media following a disciplinary hearing on 12 May. Frense was criticised for remarks she made to the *Saturday Star* newspaper criticising a radical restructuring plan which involved a repeated shuffling of programme content and times. (Freedom of Expression Institute)

On 29 May the **Media Monitoring Project** (MMP) and on 2 June the **Freedom of Expression Institute** (FXI) made submissions to the Truth and Reconciliation Commission ahead of its hearings into the role of the media under apartheid. The mainstream newspaper industry and public broadcasting corporation were sharply criticised for falling short of their role to inform the public and accused of colluding with the authorities, ostensibly to limit draconian measures, through self-censorship. (Freedom of Expression Institute)

On 9 June the Ministry of Safety and Security ordered that all current crime statistics will be released only through officially audited quarterly reports. In Northern Province where there has been a spate of violent protests by local residents of Bushbuckridge, a ban on reports to the media has been imposed by the local safety and security executive committee. (Freedom of Expression Institute)

SOUTH KOREA

Over 600 students were detained for illegal demonstrations in Seoul on 3 June. The students were attending a banned rally, called to denounce President Kim Young-sam's failure to disclose the financial details of his 1992 election campaign. (*Korean Herald*)

Recent publication: *Hidden Victims — the Long-Term Political Prisoners* (AI, May 1997, 9pp)

SRI LANKA

In late May the **Sri Lanka Broadcasting Bill** was rejected as unconstitutional by the Supreme Court of Sri Lanka. The bill would have placed the annual licensing of privately owned electronic media under the political control of a government-led authority. (Refugee Council, *The Sunday Times*)

SUDAN

The Sudanese government announced in early June that it is to release an undisclosed number of political detainees as a result of the 'political détente' characterised by the recent signing of a peace accord with rebel factions. (Sudan News Agency)

Recent publication: *Food and Power in Sudan — A Critique of Humanitarianism* (African Rights, May 1997, 372pp)

SWAZILAND

Senator Bhekimpi Dlamini, a member of the royal family, is reportedly threatening to sponsor a motion to close down the independent *Times of Swaziland* for reporting in the 12 May issue that King Mswati owes unpaid rates to Mbabane city council for a hotel he owns. Two days later the government ordered parastatal organisations to 'immediately cease dealings' with the paper. Several companies, including the railways and airline, have since withdrawn all advertising from the paper. (MISA)

SWITZERLAND

Special legislation was passed in early June granting **Christophe Meili**, a former security guard at the Union Bank of Switzerland, American residency. Since exposing an order he was given to shred Holocaust-era documents Meili and his family have received death threats. (*Financial Times*)

TAJIKISTAN

Aleksei Vasilivetsky, a correspondent for the Russian news agency **IMA-Press**, was detained on the Tajikistan-Uzbekistan border on 7 May and accused of possession of hashish. Colleagues believe that Vasilivetsky, who reportedly does not take drugs, was incriminated by officials for his reporting on the Tajik opposition movement. (CPJ)

THAILAND

On 11 June the interior minister launched the News Analysis Centre, a monitoring body set up to promote accurate reporting. The stated aims of the centre, which has already caused controversy, are to prevent any damage the media may do to the economy and close down any publication or programme found to be spreading 'false news'. (Reuters)

● ●

AYSENUR ZARAKOLU

Against the current

Aysenur Zarakolu is the head of Istanbul publisher Belge International Publishing Company. At the last count there were 17 active court cases against her and she owed US$10,000 in fines. She has been gaoled four times and tortured on one occasion. The evidence of her crime is found in her company's book list — works on the Kurds, the genocide of the Armenians, the minority Alawis and the history of the Greeks in Izmir — all taboo subjects in Turkey. Due in court at the end of this year, she spoke to Index about her life

'I was always against official ideologies, against taboo. I was arrested the first time in 1984, held in police custody for 40 days and tortured. They wanted to find a student who had been working for us. They did not find him.

'There are some subjects in Turkey which are not discussible, like the Armenian genocide. But if you want to stop genocide, you must discuss its history — as the Germans now do.

'I am not prepared to leave Turkey and live in another country. They must leave, not us. We love our country and we want to make it more democratic. It is more difficult to do from outside. We believe our work is important for everybody who wants to change the system. We want to make Turkey a real democracy, a country of different religions and races who can live together.

'I believe I am right so it is easier to deal with prison. If I doubled my work, it would be much harder. If you struggle, you must sometimes pay.

'We will go on.'

Interviewed by Penny Young

● ●

Recent publication: *Human Rights in Transition* (AI, May 1997, 22pp)

TIBET

Chadrel Rinpoche (*Index* 5/1995, 1/1996), the former abbot of Tashilhunpo monastery, was sentenced on 21 April to six years in prison for 'splitting the country' and violating state secrets, it was reported in early May. His assistant, **Champa Chung**, and a businessman, **Gyara Tsering Samdrup**, were tried alongside Chadrel and given four-year and two-year sentences respectively. All three had been held in detention since May 1995, in connection with the Panchen Lama controversy. (Tibet Information Network, *Guardian*)

Recent publication: *Three Tibetans Sentenced on Political Charges in Panchen Lama Dispute* (AI, May 1997, 6pp)

TOGO

On 1 May **Augustin Assiobo** (*Index* 2/1997, 3/1997), editor-in-chief of the weekly *Tingo Tingo*, was released from gaol after serving three months of a four-month prison sentence for defaming the Lomé fire brigade. (CPJ)

TONGA

Filokalafi Akau'ola, deputy editor of the *Times of Tonga* (*Index* 3/1996, 6/1996, 1/1997), was detained for 24 hours on 18 June and later charged with sedition following the paper's publication of a reader's letter critical of government policy. (CPJ, Pacific Islands News Association)

TUNISIA

Recent publication: *A Widening Circle of Repression* (AI, June 1997, 19pp)

TURKEY

On 30 April a court in Ankara sentenced 113 members of the Islamic **Aczmendi** sect to up to four years in prison on charges of forming an illegal group, insulting Turkey's founder Kemal Atatürk and breaking a ban on Islamic dress. (Reuters)

On 2 May a group of some 50 unidentified armed assailants entered the Istanbul studios of **Flash TV** and opened fire. The attack lasted approximately five minutes, after which the armed men fled. Although no-one was injured, the office sustained substantial damage. Reports suggest that the attack was in reaction to a live telephone interview with the fugitive organised-crime figure Alaatin Cakici aired on Flash TV the previous day. In the interview Cakici implicated the husband of the foreign minister, Tansu Ciller, in financial improprieties and suggested he had contacts with the criminal underworld. The following day, police sealed Flash TV's headquarters in Bursa and all broadcasts were suspended indefinitely on the grounds of the station's lack of a licence for its satellite connection and radio links. Flash TV has since resumed broadcasting through alternative transmission methods, but has been deprived of using its satellite links, severely curtailing its viewing audience. Further attacks on the media occurred at the offices of the daily *Hürriyet* (Freedom) when Hüseyin Vuran, a former theology student, threatened a security guard and shot a maintenance worker on 12 May; and at the **Sabah** media group building on 20 May when three unidentified individuals opened fire on the building's windows. (CPJ, Reuters, RSF)

On 3 May the Istanbul State Security Court closed down the Kurdish daily newspaper *Demokrasi* for one month and handed down a 20-month prison sentence and a fine to its editor **Ali Zeren**. The court decided an article 'After the Resistance', published in August 1996, contravened regulations on inciting racism. (Kurdistan Information Centre, Kurdistan Journalists' Association)

On 3 May the interior minister, Meral Aksener, announced that thousands of outlawed Islamic education centres would be closed down in a military-inspired crackdown against religious activism. Six days later police detained 24 Islamists in the eastern town of Bingol as they took part in an unauthorised march to protest the closure plan. Turkey's secularists believe the religious Imam Hatip schools are used as a breeding ground for activists in the ruling Islamic Welfare Party. (Reuters)

Lawyer **Hasan Dogan** was arrested on 6 May following an argument with a judge and accused of being a member of the Kurdish Workers Party (PKK). Dogan, who has been prosecuted on several occasions for his work defending alleged PKK members, denies the charge. (OMCT)

In mid-May the Ministry of Justice initiated legal proceedings against eight journalists over articles, published in April, which it deemed to be 'calls to insurrection and a coup d'état'. The journalists in question are: **Ertugrul Kurkcu** of the daily *Radikal* (*Index* 3/1997); **Necati Dogru**, **Fatih Cekirge** and cartoonist **Salih Memecan** of the daily *Sabah* (Morning); **Bekir Coskun** of *Hürriyet* (Freedom); **Mural Birsel** of the daily *Yeni Yüzyil* (New Century); **Omer Tarkan** of the daily *Posta*; and **Mustafa Basoglu** of the daily *Son Cagri* (Last Call). (RSF)

On 12 June a Turkish security court charged 49 people for protesting outside the US embassy on 7 June against a Turkish army cross-border operation in northern Iraq. The state-run Anatolian news agency said the protesters, members of leftist parties and human rights groups, had been arrested for 'assisting an outlawed organisation'. (Reuters)

UNITED ARAB EMIRATES

At the end of April the government lifted a ban on *The English Patient* after censoring five scenes which violated Islamic morals. The film, which had already been cut prior to its release in the Gulf state, was banned three days after opening when a govern-

ment official judged it to be offensive. (Reuters)

UGANDA

Freelance journalist **Betty Nambooze** of the state-owned daily *Bukedde*, was threatened with reprisals by two local officials in Mukono district on 9 May in connection with articles in the previous day's edition. Nambooze had reported the reappearance of armed men in Makono and the displacement of Kolo village residents because of plans by an investor. (CPJ)

UKRAINE

Taras Moskaliuk, host of *Ranok Vechora*, was briefly abducted on 6 June by two youths demanding that his television programme drop its use of Russian and immediately start to broadcast in Ukrainian. They threatened to blow up the station of Ukrainian TV if their requests were not met. (CPJ)

UNITED KINGDOM

Channel Four refused to show election broadcasts by the **British National Party** or the **ProLife Alliance** (*Index* 3/1997) in their entirety in late April, cutting images which it claimed were offensive to audiences. Enterprise, the Internet provider responsible for Prolife's website, also insisted that images of aborted foetuses were removed from the site. (*Independent*)

On 21 May Westminster council voted to ban the film *Crash* from the borough (*Index* 3/1997). Bans against the film remain in force in High Wycombe, Walsall and Lanarkshire. (*Independent*)

A series of books on sexuality aimed at adolescents were rejected by publisher Hodder Children's Books in early June, reportedly as a result of their inclusion of accounts of homosexual experiences. Hodder described the books as unsuitable for the UK market. (*Guardian*)

On 19 June **Helen Steel** and **David Morris**, the activists involved in the McLibel case (*Index* 2/1997), were ordered to pay US$95,000 in damages against McDonalds. The company have said they will not pursue costs from Steel and Morris to the point of their bankruptcy. (*Guardian*, Envirolink)

The (unelected) Muslim Parliament is leading a campaign to ban the Indian film *Border*, which it perceives as offensive to Muslims, it was reported in late June. The Bellevue cinema in Edgware was the subject of an arson attempt on 22 June during a late night showing of the film. (*Guardian*)

USA

On 8 May Republican Ernest Istook proposed a 'Religious Freedom Amendment' to the US Constitution. The amendment, which is opposed by civil rights organisations, would permit but not mandate school prayer and other religious expression on public property. (Reuters)

On 5 June SilverStone Software announced the release of com.Policy, a management programme that allows employers to monitor employees' computer use. (Reuters)

The Southern Baptist Convention voted in mid-June to boycott **Walt Disney** products on the grounds of the company's 'gay-friendly' policies and output, including the controversial TV comedy *Ellen*. (*Guardian*)

On 25 June Nike announced their decision to recall a range of sports shoe after a four-month dispute with the Islamic community. Muslims complained that the shoe's logo resembled the word 'Allah' in Arabic. (*Guardian*)

On 26 June the Supreme Court ruled that the 1996 Communications Decency Act was in violation of the First Amendment. The act sought to criminalise the distribution of offensive material to minors via the Internet. Many service providers already operate voluntary controls against indecency which enable parents to block unsuitable sites. (*Guardian*, PR Newswire)

WESTERN SAMOA

Savea Sano Malifa and **Fuimaono Fereti Tupua**, the publisher and an editor respectively of the daily *Samoa Observer*, were charged with libel on 18 June in connection with a letter the paper published allegedly defaming the prime minister. Two days later a change in the law was introduced to remove the paper's business licence for 'stirring up trouble'. (Pacific Islands News Association)

YEMEN

On 27 May journalists **Abdul Jabbar Saad** and **Abdullah Saad** were sentenced to 80 lashes each on charges of libel. Abdullah Saad, editor of the weekly opposition newspaper *Al-Shura*, and his brother were convicted of having written and published a series of articles criticising Sheikh Abdul Majid Zendani, a leading politician in the Al-Islah political party. The brothers were banned from journalism for one year and *Al-Shura* was ordered to cease publication for six months. (AI)

ZAMBIA

On 22 May **Fred M'membe**, **Bright Mwape** and **Masautso Phiri** (*Index* 6/1996) were acquitted of contravening the Official Secrets Act by publishing details of a cabinet plan for a referendum over the 1996 draft constitution. (MISA)

★ ★ ★

General publication: *Policing and Human Rights in the Southern African Development Community (SADC)* (AI, April 1997, 15pp)

★ ★ ★

Compiled by: Penny Dale (Africa); Victoria Millar, Sarah A Smith (Asia); Adam Newey, Sarah A Smith, Vera Rich (eastern Europe & CIS); Emily Walmsley (Latin America); Michaela Becker, Philippa Nugent (Middle East); Briony Stocker (north America & Pacific); Jessie Banfield (western Europe)

Baku, Azerbaijan: a future of promise — Credit: *Carlos Reyes/Andes Press Agency*

The high price of oil

The quest for oil goes on regardless of the rights of indigenous people, the destruction of virgin forest, the murderous habits of dictators or the pollution of the earth. The oil industry has become the whipping boy for environmental campaigners and human rights activists alike. But *Index* asks where the blame really lies: with western societies even more addicted to oil than to tobacco? Or the collusion between governments and the oil industry, greedy in their pursuit of wealth? To whom should we address our concerns?

EDWARD L MORSE

A case for oil

The oil industry has an image problem. Or is it more than that: a complete disregard for the land and the people in whose countries it operates? Whatever the case, unless the industry cleans up its act and addresses its critics, it could find itself facing regulation from outside

EXCEPT perhaps in those parts of the world where oil production has had a dramatic impact on local life — in Baku or Tulsa, Riyadh or Jakarta — the petroleum industry has failed to capture the popular imagination. Despite the fact that inexpensive fossil fuel is the foundation of modern society, feeding its industrial, commercial, residential, power and, by no means least, its transport sector, the industry that is responsible for finding, developing, refining and bringing the products to markets suffers from an image problem.

Like the tobacco industry, with which it is often compared, the oil industry suffers from a bad reputation. It is associated in the public mind with pollution. It is correlated with countries whose governments have pernicious regimes that violate human rights yet appear to be supported by foreign companies investing to develop their oil and gas resources. Its corporations appear to generate excess profits at the public's expense, and seem to be bigoted and insensitive to the needs of their employees or the indigenous populations in countries whose resources they exploit. Oil companies are often tainted by corruption. Their relationship to their own governments is often complex: at times they seem to be the tools of foreign policy; at others they appear to be unmindful of the foreign policy objectives in their governments' attempts to prevent the flow of oil from an unfriendly foreign government.

Unlike the tobacco industry, which has no social virtues yet works hard to persuade its consumers of the benefits of its products, few efforts are made to counterbalance the negative view of the petroleum sector in industrial countries by fostering an understanding of the positive attributes of the industry. Governments have not done so; nor, more surprisingly, have the companies themselves done a creditable job of portraying themselves as playing a critical, let alone an admirable role in modern industrial society. Whether in Europe or in North America, by far their most visible public image is a negative one, associated with such activities as lobbying for favourable tax treatment or against regulations that are associated with more stringent environmental standards, punctuated periodically by corporate mismanagement of a number of well-publicised events, such as the pollution associated with the Exxon Valdez spill in 1989, or Shell's insensitivity over the removal of the Brent-Spar North Sea platform in 1995.

During the past decade, public sensitivity to environmental degradation has become more acute. The oil and gas industries are under more careful scrutiny by a variety of specialised groups than ever before.

The fact that the burning of fossil fuels is having long-term effects on the hospitality of the planet has led critics, as well as more neutral observers, to ask what is the 'real' price of oil. Is it more than the US$18–22 per barrel range at which crude has been traded for most of this decade? Should the cost of cleaning up oil's environmental, political and social costs also be taken into account?

Faced by this enhanced scrutiny, a number of companies, notably British Petroleum (BP) and Royal Dutch Shell, mauled over the decommissioning of the Brent-Spar platform, the 1995 execution of Ken Saro-Wiwa and the development of the new deep-water drilling frontier northwest of the Shetlands, have begun to engage their critics in dialogue (see page 50). Both companies recently announced strategies aimed at improving their overall performance. This won a brief round of applause, but is unlikely to appease their more absolutist critics for whom the petroleum industry, like the tobacco industry, is profiteering from an evil that can only be dealt with by banishing the use of fossil fuels altogether from modern society.

Yet in general, the oil industry's response to this rising scrutiny has been muted. It is puzzling that the petroleum sector has done such a poor job in fostering the positive image that could easily be achieved if it stressed the more benevolent and productive contribution it makes to everyday life. Outside the energy industry, whether in agriculture, construction, heavy industry, computers or even the transport sector, corporate leaders are not shy about publicising and promoting — often in highly vocal ways — the ways in which their own corporate prosperity coincides with and contributes to social and economic well-being.

Yet the oil industry remains largely passive in the face of attack. Billions of barrels of oil are safely extracted and transported annually, yet a company's reputation can be torn down overnight by one accident or the killing of a single bystander. This does not happen in the airline industry, where safety standards and the costs of failure are comparable with those of the petroleum industry.

There are identifiable reasons why the industry has had such difficulty in presenting a case for itself, some of them structural. Though the most global of industries, it remains parochial and insular, particularly in the USA where a legacy of anti-trust legislation has fostered a fear among oil companies that any attempt to draw closer to one another would be seen by the government as the first step towards collusion and price-fixing. Thus when one company is confronted by a major public relations fiasco, such as an oil spill, a refinery fire or an offshore accident, offers by others to speak out in its defence are scarce. Industry-wide associations do exist, but their primary purpose is to lobby against hostile legislation rather than play the sectoral spokesman. Few corporate leaders, as a result, identify the interests of their own company with those of the industry as a whole, or see negative consequences for themselves in the plight of their competitors.

This sense of individualism, however, is married to a peculiar aversion to publicity over their oil company assets, which intensified in the 1960s with the rise of resource nationalism. Over the ensuing 20 years, two-thirds of the world's oil outside the USA and the Soviet Union was nationalised, forcing companies to look for untapped resources in the diminishing area of the world still open to their investments. In these obscure corners they discovered what one oil industry writer has called 'the obsolescing bargain', a Faustian pact in which the more that was spent on developing a strike, the more power over it would shift to the host

Right: Exxon Valdez clean-up 1989: a case of corporate mismanagement
— Credit: Heidi Bradner/Panos Pictures

government. A regime would first welcome the investment with open arms, and then promptly hold it to ransom.

Oil companies, of course, were not entirely supine, but many of their advantages were counted against them. Take size. The annual turnover of the average international major is bigger than the GDP of the developing countries in which they seek to do business. This made them potentially intimidating as investors, particularly when allied to the suspicion that they represented the foreign policy interests of their country of registration. Another disadvantage was their role as employers. They were, generally, good ones who paid rates that were considerably higher than local salaries and even the salaries of the officials who monitored their activities. But this transferred loyalties to the company from the government: they were Trojan Horses, eroding the sovereignty of the nations in which they had invested.

The oil company contractors held some trump cards. They possessed what was required — technology, human resources, professionalism and, above all, foreign capital. Illicit payments were undeniably part of the game, but so were the more legitimate ones contracted in the name of 'good citizenship'. Companies built roads and hospitals, they provided skills training, subsidised farms, invested in ancillary sectors and built facilities for sports and the arts. But they could not overstate their contribution to the host country's living standards, lest they become too closely identified with the regime in power. Even where oil companies did not engage in corrupt practice, they were the travelling companions of corrupt regimes.

This was an intractable problem in South Africa, Nigeria and the Andean states where ethnicity was, or is, a crucial ingredient in domestic politics and external critics vociferously press for oil companies to disinvest. The South African dilemma, in fact, was the least difficult to resolve in that apartheid was a unique evil, and identified as such by international bodies and the states where oil companies do most of their business. Nor was it, significantly, a major energy producer. While oil companies argued that their role as non-discriminatory providers of jobs was a positive contribution, they recognised that their position in South Africa was as untenable as that of their competitors.

Far more complex is the question of the rights of indigenous peoples to a share in oil profits and the related issue of rainforest depletion. Shell's debacle in Nigeria over the claims of the Ogoni people, and the difficulties faced by Texaco, YPF, Conoco, Occidental and BP in Colombia, Ecuador and Peru, all derive from the same basic quandary which further illustrates the theory of the 'obsolescing bargain'. Indigenous peoples and modern states differ intrinsically, and often violently, over definitions of boundary, rights and history but it is with governments that companies are forced to negotiate, even when they exert only the most cursory control over the land under discussion.

The matter of sovereignty carries less weight with the company than the guarantee of security for the investment of its shareholders. That is not, fundamentally, an ethical decision but a pragmatic choice in a high-risk business environment. The more investment expands, in the shape of drilling rigs, pipelines, refineries and shipping terminals, the more vulnerable it is to disruption and the more the investor comes to rely on the security provided by a government of disputed legitimacy. Similarly, the very act of building a supply road into a rainforest oil camp involves a devolution of control, not solely from an oil company to the national or provincial government, but from the indigenous population to an army of landless waiting at the edges of its domain. Oil company activity exacerbates these ethnic or land-use tensions by empowering one group at the expense of another and increasing the size of the stake but it is arguable whether it is directly responsible for their existence.

Rainforest depletion is the first in a series of causal links between fossil fuel extraction and climatic change which now affect oil companies at every level of operations: from the increasingly denuded Amazon; to Europe, where carbon taxes have been imposed on oil products; and in global fora, where the world is increasingly divided between industrialised and developing countries. The Kyoto conference on climate change in December will seek to address these concerns, but consensus is by no means on the horizon.

At odds are the oil producers, especially in OPEC, which regard 'green' taxes in the European Union (EU) and Japan as no more than an effort to extract 'rents' on their chief export, while the US, EU and Japan disagree as to what constitute 'reasonable' global targets for carbon emission reduction and the appropriate mechanisms for attaining them — taxes versus regulation. Oil companies are caught in the middle of this political debate. Their instinctive reaction is to use their influence with government to be obstructionist, lest the conference adopts global regulations which are inimical to their economic interests. Only BP and

Shell, both of which have suffered a poor press in recent years, have adopted policy positions that are sympathetic to environmental concerns, but that also posit the question whether the world is capable of moving away from its utter dependence on fossil fuels.

The perceived intimacy between government and oil industry interests, however, has become increasingly strained since the end of the Cold War, particularly in the USA where, for the first time since the Arab embargo of 1973-74, oil has re-emerged as a general instrument of foreign policy. While the Soviet threat loomed, the conventional wisdom in the West was that trade instruments of any kind tended to magnify the international tensions that could lead to war. Since the collapse of the Soviet Union, the international community has increasingly looked to oil as a means of enforcing its will, notably in South Africa, Libya, Iraq and Iran. While there remains reasonable debate over the effectiveness of such sanctions, there is none whatever over their legitimacy under international law.

This is highly disturbing to US oil companies and their foreign contractors, who are subject to secondary boycotts on investment, particularly in Iran and Libya — and not only because of the competitive advantage it hands to their French, Russian and Asian competitors. While US companies might be inveigled into dropping their guard over environmental issues, they deeply resent having their energy policy defined in terms of a general set of foreign policy principles, ranging from human rights violations, drug trafficking, the export of terrorism or the development of weapons of mass destruction.

As good citizens, they have to obey the law in spite of the loss of business. But if complaining about such legislation confirms the public prejudice that they are amoral and avaricious, not complaining is a frank admission to host governments that they are instruments of US foreign policy, pure and simple.

Oil is a dirty fuel. It can pollute both the physical and political environment, even with the most careful monitoring. But if the industry has come a long way in recognising that its own best interests lie in respecting safety standards, an aversion to regulation of any kind is bred in the bone. It fought the clean-up of toxic wastes, the campaigns for lower emission levels and alternative fuels, the introduction of double-hulled tankers and, currently, the disposal of obsolete exploration platforms. Rather than assuming a more proactive role as a partner of government, it has been, for the most part, its bitterest critic.

There are a few exceptions: BP, Arco in the US and Phillips Petroleum, whose promotional campaign has positioned it as a champion of strict environmental standards. But the industry, as a whole, has been appallingly slow in coming to terms with the changed priorities of its primary market, the western consumer. During the past decade of corporate downsizing, outsourcing and aggressive cost-cutting, the industry has displayed far greater concern for its short-term profitability and its appeal to investors in the City than for the justified concern of people in the street.

There were valid arguments for draconian action in the 1980s and 1990s. Unparalleled cash flows in the previous two decades had led to swollen staff numbers and a portfolio of investments well beyond the industry's core competence. A return to record levels of profitability in recent years should provide senior management with the confidence they need to take another look at their public images. They must take the opportunity to rebuild their reputation as major contributors to economic growth, as pioneers in the development and application of technologies that reinforce, rather than hinder, the attainment of public sector goals and of being good citizens as employers.

Oil companies have a good story to tell. But they need to overcome the decades of bad habits which have reinforced their reputation as nay-sayers to government and customers. Unless they do, they could become vulnerable, as public disdain at their high-handed methods combines with a wave of higher prices to create a demand for more intense regulation. This contingency is not so remote and could become frighteningly real with a single sustained disruption in the Persian Gulf or north Africa. In just such an environment, oil companies might witness a major review of the laissez-faire regime in which they have operated for decades. ❏

Edward L Morse *is publisher of the New York-based Energy Intelligence Group*

Some startling facts about oil

US dependence on foreign oil is 45%

In Nigeria oil makes up over 90% of government revenues

Twenty years of oil extraction in the Ecuadorian Amazon will keep the USA supplied at its present rate of consumption for 12.7 days

In 1995 daily demand for oil worldwide was: Asia 16.94 million barrels (25% of the world's consumption), north America 20.25, Europe 15.33, Africa 2.17

In 1995 the net oil import bill for Asia was over US$60 billion

Chinese demand for oil doubled between 1985 and 1995

Of the top 20 companies in the *Fortune 500*, five are oil companies

Ethical opposition to corporate oil companies goes back to the nineteenth century when the journalist Ida Turbell headed vociferous protests against the employment and trading practices of the first big US oil company, Rockefeller's Standard Oil

Had Saddam Hussein held on to Kuwait, he would have controlled 25% of the world's oil reserves

Chief executives of 1,400 European companies surveyed by the *Financial Times* and Price Waterhouse voted Shell 'the [European] company which deals best with environmental issues'

Shell's annual profits in Nigeria are between US$170 and 190 million

In 1995 TOTAL produced thousands of 'scratch and sniff' cards for women's magazines in France to publicise its new range of perfumed petrol

The USA dumps more than 1.4 million tonnes of used oil in landfills, on land and down sewers each year. This is equivalent to 35 Exxon Valdez disasters every year

The Mediterranean makes up only 1% of the planet's oceans but absorbs 12.5% of the world's oil spills

Between 1926 and 1947 Venezuela produced more oil than the entire Middle East

The price of oil in real terms is now lower than in 1970

Between 1982 and 1992 Shell spilt more than 6.4 million litres of oil in more than 100 countries — 40% more than the Exxon Valdez spill

President Clinton marked Earth Day by extending the US community's 'right to know' to include activities at petroleum bulk terminals such as toxic emissions: all data must be publicly available. Industry groups say the costs of the scheme far outweigh the benefits

The world has consumed nearly half the recoverable supplies of oil

The world is consuming oil three times faster than it is finding it

The world's largest oil refinery — capacity 769,500 barrels per day — is in Ulsan, South Korea

Between 1976 and 1991 official figures quote 2,976 oil spills totalling 2.1 million barrels in Nigeria, an average of almost four barrels a week

Environmental teams working to minimise damage caused by the Sea Empress oil spill off the coast of Pembrokeshire, UK, found 6,900 dead or severely damaged birds

In 1996 the UN Security Council loosened its 1990 ban on Iraqi oil sales, approving an 'oil-for-food' exchange programme for Iraq. Iraq has supplied the full amount of oil permitted under the first six months of the UN plan, but has so far only received 40% of the supplies purchased with the money

A leading Iraqi opposition group has accused Saddam Hussein's government of violating the oil-for-food deal by halting food shipments to tribes in southern Iraq who oppose the regime

A quarter of the world's known oil reserves are in Saudi Arabia yet the calorific intake of the average Saudi citizen is lower than his counterpart in oil-poor Lebanon and Jordan

No French, British or US government has ever criticised the human rights record of the oil-producing Gulf States

Between 1960 and 1980 two-thirds of the world's oil outside the West was nationalised

Sources: Project Underground; American Petroleum Institute; Oil in Asia-markets — Trading, Refining and Deregulation by Paul Horsnell; Fortune 500; The Prize by Daniel Yergin; Oxford Energy Forum; Oil and Gas Journal; Venezuela: The Political Economy of Oil by Juan Carlos Boue; Oil Watch; The World's Oil Supply, 1930-2050 by C J Campbell & J H Laherre; Catma Films; University of Wales; ArabNet; CNN Interactive; OneWorld Online; Saïd Aburish; Edward L Morse

Compiled by Jessie Banfield and Nevine Mabro

OLIVIER ROY

Crude manoeuvres

There was a time when holidays on the Caspian Sea meant caviar and casinos. Now it's boom town Baku and the oil industry has descended to fight for a slice of the action on the world's latest wild frontier

WITHIN the next 15 years, the Caspian region will become the planet's second largest source of petrol and gas after the Middle East. Its three principal producers, Azerbaijan, Turkmenistan and Kazakhstan, are already linked to the European hydrocarbons market by a network of pipelines across Russia. But the system is ramshackle and unequal to the challenge of pumping the flood of energy expected to flow from Asia's hinterland in the first decade of the twenty-first century.

More crucially, the network remains the property of largely state-owned Russian companies like Gazprom and Transneft. They have scant access to the enormous investment needed for rehabilitation but nevertheless exact a heavy toll on the transit and distribution of Caspian energy through their pipelines. The producing countries, and corporations such as Exxon, Chevron, BP and UNOCAL, which have invested heavily in regional energy development, are anxious to upgrade and, if possible, to extend the existing export network. But the development of alternative routes raises issues which are more strategic than financial.

The territory crossed by new pipelines, and the ports where they terminate will, like the Persian Gulf today, become a focal part of the security landscape of the West, the USA in particular. Regional superpowers, such as Russia and Iran, could find themselves handed a custodial role over the rest of the world's energy supply, depending on which routes are ultimately chosen. Conversely, any pipeline route that favours the region's smaller powers would entail a political commitment to resolving or defusing the conflicts which are endemic to the Caucasus,

Afghanistan and also Turkey, burdened with its Kurdish problem.

There are three feasible directions for new Caspian pipelines, each comprising a number of variant sub-routes: the European path (including Turkey), a path through the Middle East and a third in the east. The European path is the most complex, since it is divided into three separate branches, two of which already exist. Both lines terminate at the Black Sea. The first runs across the northern Caucasus from Azerbaijan through the Chechen capital of Grozny to the Russian Black Sea port at Novorossiisk. A second crosses the southern Caucasus, ending at Batumi, theoretically a Georgian port but actually controlled by Russian-backed separatists in the autonomous region of Adjaria.

The disadvantage of both pipelines is that they lead to ports which are ill-suited to supertankers and will therefore require substantial investment. Shipping congestion in the Bosphorus is another stumbling block: sooner or later, the strait will be closed to supertankers altogether. Two options remain: an extension of the pipelines under the Black Sea through Bulgaria to Greece — from where the energy can be exported by tanker through the Aegean Sea — or an overland route through Turkish Anatolia.

There are two variants on the latter proposal: either a north-south extension of the existing Georgian pipeline or an east-west route, starting in Azerbaijan and passing through Armenia. Both would terminate at Turkey's mediterranean port of Ceyhan, the terminal for oil from northern Iraq and well-equipped for supertankers.

The Middle Eastern path is exclusively Iranian and runs directly from the Caspian to energy terminals on the Persian Gulf. The eastern options are a pipeline through western Afghanistan, connecting Turkmenistan with the new Pakistani port of Gwadar on the Indian Ocean, with a spur line to supply Karachi; and another which shadows the ancient Silk Route across Kazakhstan and Sinkiang to Beijing, with an export terminal on the Yellow Sea.

Apart from the Chinese route, where the high levels of investment involved make it unrealistic at present, all the pipeline options imply choices which are above all political and strategic, rather than strictly economic. The first gamble concerns the Middle East. From a purely commercial point of view, Iran, with a single negotiating partner — the Iranian government — and no other interests within the country to accommodate, is the obvious choice for Caspian energy exporters. The country also has a well-developed infrastructure, technical expertise and a skilled workforce; its ports on the Persian Gulf have been tailored to energy industry needs and are nearest to the growing markets of southeast Asia.

The drawback, of course, is the USA's intransigent opposition to any co-operation with Iran, itself a decision more strategic than ideological. Washington's hostility is not exclusively the result of its current efforts to isolate Iran, a policy exemplified by the D'Amato law forbidding any major US investment in the country. Of equal concern is the increased dependency on the Middle East for the security of world energy supplies that pipelines through Iran would create. If the bulk of oil from the Caspian, as well as the Middle East, were to transit through the Persian Gulf, mastery over it would be more urgent than ever. Energy security would continue to depend on the western–Middle Eastern equation, one that could become in the worst scenario, an Islamist one.

The US prognosis for the Gulf is pessimistic. The possible breakdown in the Arab-Israeli peace process, the deadlock over Iraq, the tenacity of militant Islam — the product of economic under-development — fill America with alarm. But, above all, it is the fragility of the Saudi regime, whose collapse would deprive the US of a land base in the Gulf to cope with crises, that has convinced Washington not to put its new oil marbles in the Middle Eastern basket (see Saudi file *Index* 4/96).

The Afghan pipeline project, farther east, is controlled by a single company, California-based UNOCAL (see page 163), with the collaboration of DeltaOil of Saudi Arabia, and strongly supported by Turkmenistan and Pakistan. But UNOCAL may have made a serious miscalculation by staking all on a single player in the Afghan conflict — the Taliban. In autumn 1995, the highly conservative movement seized control of western Afghanistan, the route of UNOCAL's proposed pipeline from Turkmenistan to the Indian Ocean. A visit to the region, organised by Pakistan's former interior minister, General Nasirullah Babar, who was accompanied — in defiance of all diplomatic conventions — by the US ambassador to Pakistan, was a clear indication of the choices made by Washington and Islamabad.

Having successfully evicted an Argentine rival, BRIDAS, already working on a trans-Afghan pipeline, UNOCAL signed two agreements with the Turkmen government in 1995 and 1996. But the capture of Kabul by the Taliban on 26 September 1996 did not bring the expected breakthrough. Exclusively Pashtun, the Taliban have since encountered stiff resistance from other Afghan minorities, notably the Uzbeks, Tajiks and Hazaras. The 'students of religion' received their heaviest setback in June 1997, when their forces were driven south into the Hindu Kush. Meanwhile, UNOCAL is pushing ahead with the project — a US$2 billion gas line, later to be twinned with an oil pipeline.

The export direction favoured by all other western companies, except UNOCAL, is, by elimination, to Europe through the Caucasus. This would give a key role in energy security to Moscow but also poses some fundamental questions about political stability, not only in the Caucasus but in Russia itself.

A series of accords in October 1996 and March 1997 between the members of the Caspian Petroleum Corporation (CPC) resulted in the launch of a new Kazakhstan-Novorossiisk oil pipeline, backed by LUKoil, Transneft and Rosneft (Russia), Arco (USA) and Shell. Chevron, Agip, Mobil, Oryx and British Gas were all expected to subscribe, Amoco has put up the capital share of the Kazakh government, which it is incapable of paying. The pipeline, due to be completed by the end of 1999, will transport an estimated 1.5 million barrels of oil per day. In a parallel development, meanwhile, the international consortia working in Azerbaijan have shown a preference for modernising the existing pipelines, which pass through Chechnya or Georgia, respectively.

All three schemes require a fundamental clarification of the role of Russia which, up to now, has behaved more like an adversary than a partner in the development of the region's energy potential. A military doctrine of 1993 defined the former frontiers of the Soviet Union as a continuing zone of security for the Russian Federation, whose policies in those regions asserted a form of territorial and military neo-imperialism through the formation of the Commonwealth of Independent States (CIS). Countries that had become nominally independent after the collapse of the Soviet Union in 1991 remained shackled by bilateral agreements, linking military co-operation (the presence of Russian bases, Russian control of international frontiers, integrated command), economic co-operation (customs agreements) and continuing subordination (Russian monopoly of the network of gas and oil pipelines).

Russia 'commercialises' Turkmen gas by fixing its price, imposing quotas and interrupting at will export routes and barter agreements to advance its own economic interests. In 1996 Russia restricted Kazakh exports to just 4-5 million tonnes of petrol and, in October, cut off the supply of electricity to the entire north of the republic on the grounds that the government had not settled its debts. The charge was not without foundation, but it could be explained in large measure by Russia's embargo on Kazakh trade. Similarly, under pretext of the conflict in Chechnya, Moscow blocked the transport of Azeri oil north through Dagestan.

In the early 1990s Moscow had actively encouraged conflicts in the Caucasus while presenting itself as an honest broker between the combatants. It openly supported the Ossetian, Abkhazian and Adjarian minorities in their rebellions against Georgia and provided military aid to the Armenians in the war with Azerbaijan over Nagorno-Karabakh. Russian mercenaries also fought alongside the Azeris. Despite its transparent involvement, Russia still shared the presidency of the Minsk

Taliban in Kabul, 1996: God, guns and pipelines — Credit: Chris Steele-Perkins/Magnum Photos

Group, charged with resolving the conflict (see page 74).

The limits of this policy were very soon apparent to Russia's more liberal economists. Such peremptory blocks on the Muslim republics could only provoke them to break with Moscow altogether and turn to the USA, as both Azerbaijan and Uzbekistan have done, while seeking alternative routes for their energy exports. The war in Chechnya had exposed the hollowness of the Russian military threat. The Central Bank, meanwhile, had deprived Moscow of a lever of monetary influence by expelling all other CIS members from the rouble zone. There was little left to be gained from insisting on a transport monopoly of the region's energy if no-one was investing in its production.

Finally Russian energy companies, such as LUKoil, aspired to reinvent themselves as multinational corporations, standing shoulder-to-shoulder with Chevron and Exxon, rather than playing a passive role as the economic weapon of an outdated colonialism. In the course of 1996, the authorities adopted a different strategy. Rather than block western companies, the Russians would allow them to make the investments that they could not afford themselves, prior to proposing (or imposing) their own participation in the transport end of the energy equation, under terms acceptable to the international companies. As a result, last year Moscow distanced itself from the Abkhazian cause, mended fences with Azerbaijan and held peace negotiations in Tajikistan. LUKoil, under its president Vagit Alekperov (a Russian, ironically, of Azeri origin) skipped off to play in the garden of the Seven Sisters — the Anglo-Saxon multinationals.

In the eyes of the West, Russia at last seemed less unpredictable and predatory. Its involvement as a partner in efforts to develop the Caspian hub was preferable to turning the region into another Middle East and was taken as a pledge of Russia's commitment to international co-operation at a time when the enlargement of NATO had made it profoundly nervous.

Until that turning-point, energy experts had watched the growth of a Russo-Iranian axis in Central Asia, one that was opposed to any western penetration of the former USSR. Russia and Iran have some interests in common. The first concerns the legal status of the Caspian. For Moscow and Tehran, it is a lake while Azerbaijan, strongly supported by the USA and more discreetly by Turkmenistan, regards it is an inland sea. The stakes are clear: if the Caspian is a lake, then its resources would have to be divided equally among the surrounding states, whatever the extent of their territorial waters. If it is a sea, its resources would be divided according to a state's territorial waters, which are determined by projecting the length of a nation's littoral out into the Caspian.

For obvious reasons Russia and Iran, which occupy the two narrow ends of the great rectangle which is the Caspian, argue in favour of a lake; Azerbaijan is for marine status, which would give it the bulk of the offshore reserves. Kazakhstan and Turkmenistan are instinctively pro-sea but, for political reasons, have been forced into the pro-lake camp. On 12 November 1996 Russia, Iran, Turkmenistan and Kazakhstan signed a protocol in Ashgabat affirming that the territorial waters of the Caspian states extended only 45 miles into the Caspian waters, the remainder of which would be exploited in a consortium. Azerbaijan has refused to sign.

Russia and Iran share other ties. These include support for Armenia, a desire to punish Azerbaijan for its drift to the West, a joint hostility to the rise of the Taliban in Afghanistan and last but not least, Russian arms sales to Iran. With Iran's withdrawal of its support for the Islamist opposition in Tajikistan in 1994 — with whom the Russians in any case negotiated in 1996 — the two countries had little to fight about.

The rapprochement between Russia and the West over energy-related issues has led to a realignment of other regional alliances. One symptom has been the changing attitude of Turkey, until now alarmed by the prospect of Moscow eventually returning in force to the southern Caucasus. Turkey had already recognised the weakness of its much-vaunted pan-Turkic policy, which had shaped its diplomacy among the Turkic-speaking peoples of the Caucasus and Central Asia since 1991. Relations with Azerbaijan and Georgia had soured, chiefly as a result of the bizarre conspiracy — much deplored by diplomats — between the Turkish mafia and its secret services to provide support to the political opponents of Azeri President Heydar Aliyev and to Georgia's Adjarian separatists.

Ankara had further realised that, linguistic links notwithstanding, 90 per cent of its CIS trade was with Russia and the Ukraine, not the Muslim republics and that, far from being the bridgehead of the West's penetration of Central Asia that it had supposed, the multinationals had no need whatsoever of Turkish intermediaries. If Turkey wanted Caspian oil and gas to transit through its territory, it had better co-operate with Russia. The major obstacle for the Turks, however, is that any land-based pipeline through the Caucasus has to cross the Kurdish provinces in the southeast (an alternative pipeline has been proposed to the Black Sea port of Samsun, but would require a marine connection). In January 1997, an attack by the Kurdistan Workers Party (PKK) on the Iraqi pipeline to Ceyhan sent a clear message to Ankara: only a political resolution of the Kurdish question would ensure the security of the pipelines.

Iran, anxious to preserve good relations with Moscow at a time when there was no sign of a softening in Washington's stance, also recognised that Russo-Iranian interests had diverged. Tehran has no desire to see either the Caucasian or Afghan pipelines successfully built and was badly disappointed that Russia supported US insistence that it be excluded from the Azeri pipeline consortium. In short, if business is increasingly the name of the new Great Game in Moscow, in Tehran it is still dominated by the fear of eventual encirclement by the US, Saudi Arabia and Turkey.

In the absence of a grand alliance with Russia, Iran has launched a softly-softly policy towards the states of Central Asia, notably Turkmenistan and Kazakhstan, to prove that it provides the only credible economic solution to their inaccessibility. This policy has suffered cruelly from the US embargo on foreign investment. The last section of a trans-Iranian railway, linking Turkmenistan to the Indian Ocean, was opened with great ceremony in May 1996, but remains largely symbolic. The railway will transport part of Turkmenistan's 1.5 million tonne cotton crop and a little aluminium from Tajikistan, but even those operations require a heavy investment in rolling stock.

But the pace of Iranian commercial diplomacy has accelerated. In August 1996 Turkey's Islamist prime minister, Necmettin Erbakan, and President Ali Akbar Hashemi Rafsanjani of Iran announced the construction of a US$7 billion gas pipeline from Tehran to Ankara to meet domestic Turkish demand. Iran has also multiplied its swap arrangements, enabling Kazakhstan and Turkmenistan to earn a reasonable price for gas piped through existing lines to northern Iran, where the majority of the Iranian population live. Tehran matches the supply with surplus from its southern gas fields, which it sells on the world market and credits to the accounts of its northern neighbours.

Iran must on no account be cancelled out of the Caspian equation. ❏

Olivier Roy is head of research at the CNRS, Paris

Translated by Michael Griffin

EMILY WALMSLEY

Company rules

Ecuador's Secoya Indians opt for oil, but find the pay-off doesn't live up to the promises

IN APRIL 1996 Elias Piaguaje, an Indian from the Amazon jungle of Ecuador, wrote a letter to the chief executive of Occidental Petroleum Corporation. 'As president of the Secoya people,' it began, 'I would like to inform you that we have decided to prevent any further activity by Occidental that may affect our territories.' Only a year later, at their Ninth Annual Congress, the Secoya reversed this decision by voting four to one in favour of oil exploration on their land. Within a week, 11 of their leaders had gone to the capital, Quito, to negotiate a compensation fee with Occidental. Three days later, exploration had begun.

I met the Secoya delegation off the bus from Quito the day after they signed a deal with 'the company', as they refer to Occidental. They arrived at sunrise in Shushufindi, a town created by the oil industry that now serves as the last stopping-point before the jungle. A fat, rusty pipeline snakes along the main street, heading north to join the Sistema del Oleoducto Trans-Ecuatoreano as it sets off over the mountains and down to the sea for export. Half the government budget flows out of Ecuador's Amazon along this single tube: virtually none of the government spending is brought back for reinvestment in the region. The roads in Shushufindi are unsurfaced and run freely with sewage, the air is thick with fumes, the flames from the oil stations leap high above the rooftops — the only source of light after nightfall. A white face is not welcome here: passers-by glare and mutter about thieves and murderers. Young ocelots snarl and spit on the ends of chains. I entered the town from the north, in an open-air *ranchero* bus that shuddered each time it hit a pothole and skidded along the oil-coated road in between. An old lady wedged in beside me was amazed that I dared to make my visit alone. 'The Bible said hard times

would be sent to try us,' she murmured as we approached the town. 'Well here they are, right here in Shushufindi.'

I arrived the night before the Secoyas and spent the following dawn nervously pacing the shadowy streets, hoping to intercept them as they stepped off the bus. I had met none of the group before but in the end it was easy to spot them. Their shirts were ill-fitting and rumpled, half undone in the jungle heat, they carried hardly a bag between them, and it was clear from their expressions that they did not belong in this town. Elias Piaguaje stood out immediately as the natural leader. He is small and compact with sharp eyes and a confident stride. He carried a pen in his shirt pocket and clasped a folder of documents in his hand. 'We've had a rough ride,' he said wearily, taking me by the arm. 'But now comes the roughest ride of all: telling our people that the company won't give them half the things they asked for — not even half.'

The Secoya are one of eight indigenous groups affected by oil development in the Oriente, Ecuador's Amazon region. A single clan of uncontacted Huaorani are the only Indians who remain untouched. In the past, some groups have been wiped out altogether by the industry; others, like the Cofán, have had their numbers drastically reduced. But oil companies all over the world are now claiming to have overcome this disregard for local communities and to have entered into relationships of mutual benefit. Occidental is one such and, over the last year, the Secoya have been facing a critical decision: should they fight to keep oil development off their land, or heed the company's litany of social development projects and unrivalled environmental standards? In their vote at the Annual Congress, they had succumbed to visions of the latter.

Oil production in the Oriente funds nearly half Ecuador's government budget and in only 25 years the entire region has been opened up to the industry. 'It's another Midwest out there,' says Andy Drumm, a Welsh ecologist who has worked as a tour guide in the area for nearly 10 years. The operations cannot be stopped, but environmental campaigning, highlighted by the US$1 billion lawsuit against Texaco (see page 160), has forced oil companies to adopt a green language, if not greener techniques, and to reconsider the local people as stakeholders in the development of their homelands. Paulina Garzón, who heads the anti-oil campaign at Acción Ecológica, a Quito-based non-governmental organisation, is

Left: Friendship hairdressers in Lago Agrio — Credit: Emily Walmsley

sceptical about the apparent improvements. 'The changes are totally superficial,' she claims. 'Pure PR aimed at mitigating resistance.' Nevertheless, the days of Texaco's bulldozing approach are over and the multinationals are negotiating their way into the jungle through subtler means.

The rainforest in Ecuador is owned at three different levels. The subsurface minerals belong to the state, the exploration and production rights to the oil companies, and the land — at least parts of it — belongs to the local people. As this third degree of ownership is gradually recognised, the politics of the jungle have become a mesh of complicated agreements between *petroleros*, the name for anyone working in oil, and Indian villages. In their contracts with the Ecuadorian government, oil companies are bound to more environmental and social regulations than in any other South American country. But on the ground, far from the mountain capital, the *petroleros* monitor themselves.

Occidental, generally known as Oxy, says it is proud of its relations with the local inhabitants of Block 15, the 500,000-acre concession in the northeastern Oriente where the company has operated since 1985. The company's community outreach programmes at its main site at Limoncocha, a silvery lake that once crawled with alligators, include a coffee co-operative, chicken runs, tree nurseries, and a rudimentary health centre. Manuel Echeverría, the community and public relations manager, explained the reason for these 'good works'. 'If we didn't have the consent of the local people, we simply couldn't work here. They are the land owners so they must receive some benefits. In the first stage of exploration we offer them basic needs — outboard motors, cooking stoves, roofing. If we find oil, we establish longer-term social projects.'

Oxy does not rent land from the communities; it compensates them for the company's presence. 'The ecologists say we are a corrupting influence,' Echeverría continues, 'but unlike our critics, we don't patronise the Indians. We don't study them or tell them how best to develop themselves. We just give them what they want.' Echeverría, a poised man in his mid-thirties, who commutes with ease from his Quito office to the steaming camp at Limoncocha, was once an Oxy engineer. Three years ago he became fascinated by community relations and decided to move departments. What happens, I asked him, if a village does not want the projects that Occidental offers and refuses the company access to their land? 'We wait,' he replied. 'They always come round in the end.'

The Secoya live in three communities along the south of the Aguarico river. When they moved there in the 1960s, the river was bordered by pristine jungle on either side. Now almost the entire length of its banks, from the Andean foothills down to Peru, have been cultivated, mostly by *colonos*, land-hungry immigrants from the

Elias Piaguaje, Secoya leader and negotiator in Shushufindi

mountains and the coast who followed the roads built by the oil industry. The Secoya were granted title to 40,000 hectares of land in 1989. They immediately made a hunting reserve out of the remaining stretch of virgin jungle within their territory. 'No-one was allowed to build their home within the reserve,' Elias explained. 'We live from the hunting and it was the only place where the animals were left undisturbed. But this is the area that the company wants to explore.'

The river flows due east past the largest Secoya village, San Pablo de Kantesiayá. The evening I arrived there, on the day the leaders began negotiations in Quito, the water turned black in the setting sun. A hundred kilometres upstream is Lago Agrio, a shanty town like Shushufindi, hemmed in by rusty pipelines and dripping pumps. The site of Texaco's first oil wells, it was nicknamed 'bitter lake' by the workers. Arriving by river, the first sign of San Pablo is a cluster of women washing clothes and children fishing from the muddy bank. 'It's called the rich water river,' said Manuel, who had brought me downstream in his canoe, 'but God knows what these fish have in them after swimming past Lago Agrio'.

The Secoya held out against Occidental for over a year: most local communities sign agreements with the *petroleros* within a few months. Echeverría admitted to me that they had been 'by far the hardest group yet'. One of the major obstacles faced by the company was the abiding respect that the Indians have for their leaders, many of whom, having grown up with Texaco's operations just upriver, can talk for hours about the negative impact of the oil industry. Those who speak most fluently about a future free of *petrolero* neighbours, however, are also the Secoya with the most income. Elias, for example, insists on the importance of the hunting reserve for Secoya heritage: he was also educated and supported for years by the Summer Institute of Linguistics, the evangelical missionaries who lived with the Secoya for 40 years. He owns cattle, trades coffee, travels abroad ('but the NGOs pay the ticket') and educates two children in Quito.

Most Secoya do not have Elias's wealth or long-term vision. Traditionally, their outlook on life is simply to live for the moment: the Secoya language has no words for numbers. Like other indigenous people throughout the Amazon, they are living on the frontier between jungle traditions and multinational capitalism. Miguel Angel Cabodevilla, a Capuchin priest, has lived in the Oriente since the 1970s and watched the Indians slip into this limbo. 'The Aguarico river has been opened up rapidly over the last 15 years,' he explained when I met him in the cool Quito mission. 'The Secoya's confrontation with outside forces has been sudden and confusing. They have been offered development projects from the palm oil industry, logging companies, missionaries, ecologists, NGOs, tour guides and now by oil companies too.'

Lacking any kind of welfare support from the government, the Indians have tended to choose whichever project offers them the most rewards most immediately. In the end, however, neither one nor the other is pursued wholeheartedly, leaving most Secoya with very little income, but with far greater aspirations. The Capuchin frowned: 'They have reached their most vulnerable stage of existence.'

Occidental has brought all its resources to bear on convincing the Secoya that their lives will improve if they allow the company onto their land. In February nine Oxy men and Jorge Trujillo, a local anthropologist, attended a Secoya meeting in Seguaya, a village just down river from San Pablo. Trujillo had studied the Secoya previously and explained to them how the company's management plan for the protection of their land would 'bring together the traditional knowledge of their ancestors and the help of those who can bring another type of knowledge'. The Secoya were not impressed. 'The company has adopted a very deep strategy using anthropologists,' said Colón Piaguaje, the president of San Pablo. 'I am concerned that Trujillo is here. He took a lot of information from my grandparents and now he's trying to tell us how to develop.' At the end of the meeting there was a majority vote to keep Occidental off their land.

San Pablo: Secoya Indian Matilde Payaguaje and her granddaughter — Credit: Emily Walmsley

In March, 10 Secoya were invited to the Oxy site at Limoncocha so they could see how clean the operations were and how the company had become 'part of the community' there. Teodoro, who runs tourist cabins near San Pablo, went on the tour and told me that he 'didn't see any pollution and the social projects looked great'. Elias said: 'All 10 came back sick.'

In April Echeverría took a selection of Secoya leaders to the coast for a few days. When I asked if this was a necessary part of community relations, he replied: 'They had never seen the sea. They asked us to take them, so we booked rooms on the tenth floor of a beach hotel to give them the best possible view.' Elias was not invited on this trip, nor was Colón. The company gathered that they were the millionaires of the community and could afford their own holiday. But Javier Piaguaje, the new president of the Secoya people and only a 'medium-millionaire', was taken along. I did not have a chance to meet Javier: 'He's a great guy,'

● ●

A wealth of problems

Petroecuador hoarding: 'our motto is production and environmental protection

Everyone in Ecuador recognises the red and white star of Texaco. In the 1970s, when oil first gushed from the rainforest, the logo was a reminder of new-found wealth. Today, it is seen as the symbol of pollution, degradation and destruction. Mention the current state of Ecuador's jungle and the response is always, 'Texaco's fault'.

Texaco was the first company to find rich deposits of crude in the Oriente and, until its contract ended in 1990, remained the dominant consortium operating in the area in partnership with the state oil company, Petroecuador. Since the first discoveries in 1967, development has continued more or less unregulated. 'The Oriente's booming oil industry has operated with virtually no environmental and public health controls,' says Judith Kimerling, an environmental lawyer whose ground-breaking study, *Amazon Crude*, first drew attention to the issue at the end of the 1980s.

For 20 years, no-one outside noticed that millions of gallons of oil were being spilled into the rainforest, that cheaper, substandard machinery was consistently in use, that one group of Indians had disappeared altogether and others were drastically diminishing in size. Finally, in 1993, a group of New York lawyers filed a US$1 billion class action suit against Texaco on behalf of 30,000 people living in the Oriente. The plaintiffs have accused the company of ruining their lands and rivers, causing widespread devastation to the rainforest environment and creating a dramatically increased risk of cancer for all the inhabitants of the region. 'If Texaco had operated in the US as they did in Ecuador, they would have been prosecuted for crime instantly,' says Cristóbal Bonifaz, the Ecuadorians' lead attorney.

The plaintiffs insist on suing Texaco in a US court because the damage inflicted on the rainforest resulted from technical decisions taken in the company's US offices. Texaco claims that the case should be resolved in Ecuador. 'The issues concerned and the parties involved are all in that country. Our operations were conducted by Texpet, a subsidiary company registered in Ecuador and therefore subject to Ecuadorian law,' says Yorick Fonseca, a spokesman from the New York headquarters. Texaco also claim to have completed a sufficient clean-up operation in the Oriente following an agreement with the Ecuadorian government in 1995. A recent report by the environmental unit of Petroecuador suggests it was a sham: 'Texaco has dealt with only 139 of the 632 waste pits that they left behind,' says Iván Narváez, manager of the unit. 'Their idea of cleaning up was simply to remove the waste from these pits and dump it into six new, enormous pits which now hold 80,000 barrels of toxic crude.' According to Fonseca, 'There are pits and there are pits. We only sought to close those no longer necessary for operations.'

In November 1996 the third judge appointed to the bench, Jed Rakoff, suddenly dismissed the suit on the grounds that the Ecuadorian government did not want it to take place. Ecuador's President Abdalá Bucaram reacted by publicly pledging his support for the case. 'This is the first time a sovereign state has intervened in a private lawsuit in the US to protect its citizens,' says Henry Dahl, a Texan lawyer then representing the Ecuadorian government. Despite attempts by the US ambassador, Leslie Alexander, to persuade him to do otherwise, Bucaram's successor, Fabián Alarcon, confirmed the state's support at the end of April this year. Judge Rakoff has yet to respond.

Manuel Silva, the director of La Frente por la Defensa de la Amazonia, which represents the plaintiffs in the Oriente, is optimistic that the case will eventually succeed. 'It will be the first time in history that a US-based multinational has been held accountable in a US court for its actions abroad,' he says. A victory for the plaintiffs, however, will not necessarily ensure that Texaco repairs all the damage for which it is responsible. 'The lawsuit is just one tool to be used against them,' says Judith Kimerling. 'In the long run, they will have to be shamed into cleaning up properly.' Pending a decision, the case has been instrumental in persuading foreign companies operating in Ecuador to invest far more in environmental and social programmes than previously.

The exception is Petroecuador. 'Our pipelines are like clogged arteries but we have no money to replace them,' says Pietro Mazzillo, head of reforestation at Petroecuador. 'Texaco left them behind in this state, so Texaco should put in the new ones.'

Meanwhile, María Aguinda, the first name on the list of plaintiffs, has died of cancer. *EW*

● ●

Echeverría assured me, 'young, but *tiene pilas* — raring to go.'

A month later Echeverría and his assistants turned up at the critical Ninth Annual Congress. After three days of debate, only 20 per cent of the Secoya were still opposed to the company. Whatever the Oxy men said, they seem, finally, to have convinced them.

It was hard to find a Secoya who would speak about it. Only at breakfast on the day I returned up river did José, the owner of the hut I stayed in, tell me that the company had offered each family water pumps, solar panels, fridges, fish ponds, cooking stoves. 'And that's only for the exploration stage,' he said with gleaming eyes. 'If they find oil, we'll make another deal. So stage one, we'll have a smarter house, stage two, we'll have a house each, and stage three? We'll all have palaces!' He threw up his hands in glee. He would be disappointed by the reduced number of plastic water tanks and the absence of fridges and chainsaws — 'We're an ecological company,' an Oxy man had said, 'you think we'd give you machines to cut down trees?' — the leaders had secured in their negotiations in Quito, but they did, at least, include a couple of solar panels with computers attached — useful if the company finds oil and they have to write down a second list of compensation requirements.

If oil is found on their land, the Secoya have been promised a number of programmes such as fish pools, a carpentry workshop and a machine to husk rice. Such contributions may balance out the loss of food from the hunting reserve, but they are unlikely to produce large profits that will change the Secoyas' lives. The extensive lists of *cosas* — 'things' — that each village requested from the company do not amount to a long-term development plan and nowhere in the final contract does it mention the cost of maintaining these *cosas*. Instead of becoming stronger and more independent, the Secoya could well follow the example of other communities treated in this way and start relying on the company's patronage for all their needs. Meanwhile, the compensation fee will hardly dent Occidental's budget which, like that of all good oil companies, is geared to produce as much oil as possible, as quickly as possible, at the least cost possible. ❏

Emily Walmsley is a researcher and writer specialising in Latin America

• •

NEVINE MABRO

Profile of a high stakes roller

The rise of the Union Oil Company of California from bit player to big gambler in the energy game is one of the more intriguing developments on the global scene

On 25 March 1997 Judge Richard Paez of Los Angeles made a landmark ruling on the responsibility of oil companies toward the citizens of those countries in which they were working. His judgment, in a case brought by 15 Burmese plaintiffs, held Union Oil Company of California (UNOCAL) liable for human rights violations in Burma if it could be found to have 'conspired' with the Burmese government 'to deprive plaintiffs of international human rights in order to further their financial interests in the Yadana gas pipeline project'. The US$1 billion UNOCAL-Burma joint venture in the Yadana offshore gas field is the biggest single foreign investment project since Burma's ruling military aborted the 1990 election victory of the National League for Democracy (NLD).

While the Burmese government and the Myanmar Oil and Gas Company (MOGE) escaped liability on the grounds of sovereign impunity, UNOCAL could face compensation claims for human rights abuses that allegedly occurred during construction of the pipeline. These include forced labour, torture, rape, environmental damage and the laundering of drug money.

The drug-laundering charge was made in December 1996 by the Paris-based GeoPolitical Drugwatch who accused UNOCAL's business partner, MOGE, of being the main conduit for laundering the military's heroin revenues. Robert E Wages, chairman of the 90,000-strong Oil, Chemical and Atomic Workers International Union (OCAW); has called on UNOCAL to 'clean up its dirty international business' and carry out its own investigation into the allegations. The charge is still being investigated.

President Clinton's unilateral trade sanctions on Burma are another blow to UNOCAL. While other companies have started to pull out of the country, UNOCAL's chairman, Roger Beach, expressed concern at the damage sanctions will do to Burma's economic development.

UNOCAL, the twelfth biggest oil company in the world with, according to its 1996 annual report, total revenues of US$5.3 billion, is involved at every stage of the oil chain from exploration to downstream operations. Among its claims to fame is the invention of super-refined 'clean' petrol for the demanding home market in California.

UNOCAL was founded in Santa Paula, California, in 1890, and moved into the international arena in the 1960s. Of late, it has become a high-stakes player on the international scene, particularly in the Caspian arena. Other interests include China, Afghanistan and the Democratic Republic of Congo (former Zaire), and investments in Burma, Thailand, Pakistan and the UK. It has recently set up headquarters in Kuala Lumpur, Malaysia, and says it plans 'aggressive expansion' into Asia.

In its efforts to be a key player in the area being dubbed 'the new Middle East' UNOCAL, discreetly backed by Washington, is involved in some complex political manoeuvres in Central Asia. As part of the Baku-based oil consortium Azerbaijan International Operating Company (AIOC), it already controls 9.5 per cent of the Azeri, Chirag and Guneshli fields in Azerbaijan (see page 147). Negotiations for an 'oil swap' with Iran to get Azerbaijan's oil and gas out via that country — despite the US sanctions on dealings with Iran — are under way; it is the leading contender for construction rights on a 900-mile, US$2.5 billion gas pipeline project to transport gas from southeastern Turkmenistan to the port of Gwadar in Pakistan. The proposed pipeline runs through Taliban-held areas of Afghanistan, but the renewed uncertainties of Afghanistan's civil war, and its exclusive relationship with the 'students of religion' could yet upset UNOCAL's plans.

UNOCAL's 'humanitarian assistance' to the Taliban — notably in the form of fax machines — has not, however, rendered them immune to the shifting loyalties of Afghanistan's tribal warfare. The Taliban see the pipeline deal as their route to political legitimacy and international recognition as the government of Afghanistan. Renewed conflict and the surprise retreat of the Taliban in northern Afghanistan now threaten the stability promised by their lightning conquest of two-thirds of the country. UNOCAL, all of whose eggs are in the lap of the Taliban, are currently unable to raise the cash for the pipeline on nervous international markets. While it hesitates, the Taliban are playing the field and are currently negotiating with the Argentine oil company BRIDAS. UNOCAL, however, are hoping that their 'strategic partnership' with the Saudi-owned DeltaOil and Nimir Petroleum, may yet win the Taliban over.

Should UNOCAL decide the odds in Burma are too heavily stacked against it to risk the international opprobrium this would bring, it may well choose to withdraw from there to save the bigger stake in Central Asia. Now that Burma has been admitted to the Association of Southeast Asian Nations (ASEAN), there is no shortage of Pacific companies willing to buy out its stake there.

SAÏD ABURISH

The wounds of oil

**Instead of fuelling the development of democratic institutions
and a system capable of coping with the consequences of its
new-found wealth, oil in the Middle East has weakened or
destroyed traditional religious, family and tribal adherences.
Class differences are sharper and the divide between the 'oil
chiefs' and their followers deeper today than ever**

I N THE 1930s and 1940s the oil companies became the primary
expression of the western presence in the Arab Middle East and western
policy shifted from signing treaties aimed at indirect control of the area to
doing the same through backing the biggest oil-well owners. Western oil
companies, in co-operation with their governments, supported kings and
sheikhs — the well owners — as a barrier against the people's attainment
of political rights; these they considered a danger to the oil concessions.

The story of the oil concessions reveals a consistent pattern of
conspiracy to deny the people of the oil-producing countries their human
rights because the oil companies considered democracy, freedom and the
satisfaction of the economic needs of the average Arab inimical to their
interests. As a result, oil companies operating in Saudi Arabia, Kuwait and
Bahrain paid the money from oil income into the personal accounts of
the rulers or ruling families. In the Saudi Arabia of the late 1940s, the
budget of the royal garages was three times the combined budget of the
ministries of health and education —US$4.8 million against US$1.5. A
short time later, in the 1950s, the formation of labour unions by the Saudi
workers of the ARAMCO oil consortium led to the wholesale
imprisonment of hundreds of them and the disappearance of many.

In addition to depositing oil income in personal accounts and standing
in the way of labour unions and other forms of popular expression, the
discriminatory policies of the oil companies and their governments took

on more subtle forms. In the countries above as well as in the United Arab Emirates, the oil companies used funds allocated 'to educate the local population' to favour the sons of members of the local patriarchies; while they were sent to universities, more deserving people were denied education. Many of those so favoured were incompetents: some spent 10 years obtaining bachelor's degrees; most did little to merit their qualifications and didn't work after graduating.

The same calculated policies of the oil companies extended to employment. Their close co-operation with the CIA and MI6 produced a dependence on the latter for information about would-be employees. People who expressed the gentlest form of social consciousness were denied work. This applied to individual cases as well as to whole communities whose members were unacceptable to local government. This was the case, for instance, with the Shia in Saudi Arabia (in whose territory oil was first discovered) and the Bidoon in Kuwait.

To understand the role of the oil giants in denying the people of the oil-producing countries their political and human rights, we must consider the traditional tribal system from which the ruling families of these countries sprang. Contrary to the notion which claims it was inherently dictatorial, the ruling families relied on the notion of *shura*, consultation, for survival. There was a consultative council in Saudi Arabia in the 1920s, but it disappeared in 1932 to reappear toothless in 1994: the King decreed that the *shura* council should discuss only matters referred to it. The Kuwaiti royals dissolved parliament in 1982 because they objected to its members' commitment to open debate, general accountability and protection of citizens' rights. The Emirates, Bahrain and Oman do not tolerate public discourse, and human rights organisations have documented the arbitrary punishment of violators. Contrary to the situation in China and other parts of the world, oil interests preclude censure of these misdeeds by western governments.

In all Middle Eastern oil-producing countries the rulers have isolated themselves from their people. Dependent as they are on oil income to perpetuate their rule, they see no need to accommodate any form of democracy nor to pay attention to human rights. Their income comes from the oil companies and not from a structured economic system which would foster accountability towards their people. A Saudi prince-governor of a province summed up his attitude towards his constituency by declaring: 'They are a combination of apes and slaves.'

Oil fires, Kuwait, 1991: when the West went to war for oil
— Credit: Mohamed Ansar/Camera Press

Indeed most positions of power in the oil-producing countries are held by members of the ruling families and the attitude of the Saudi prince-governor is not unusual. Princes, ministers, governors and generals in all these countries are above the law: many go as far as dissolving Islamic law courts when the judges object to their ways. Most educated people are under constant secret police surveillance; private property is often confiscated; a common thief has greater rights than a political dissenter.

The concentration of power in the hands of the ruling families and the absence of controls on their behaviour — both made possible through connivance with the oil companies — have led to massive distortion in wealth distribution and a breakdown in the social system. All members of ruling families are multi-millionaires and there are over 50 billionaires among members of the House of Saud. Meanwhile, according to the Food and Agriculture Organization of the United Nations, the calorific intake of the average Saudi citizen is lower than his counterpart in oil-poor Lebanon and Jordan. While the Saudi situation is an extreme case, the divide between rich and poor in the other oil-producing countries is also huge.

The massive discrepancy between the conditions of rulers and the ruled has produced a hybrid culture. Beyond the royal families there exists a small class of beneficiaries who are beholden to them and who buttress their refusal of the just demands of the majority of the people. Merchants, bureaucrats and army and security officers, the possessors of what might be called a 'petro-personality' fashioned by rulers and the oil companies, they constitute a minority group of loyalists whose privileged position is dependent on their creators. Mostly western-educated and visible, this group endows the oil-producing countries with superficial legitimacy which is accepted by the western world. In reality, they are nothing but cultural half-breeds who speak Arabic and English badly and fit into neither Arab nor western social moulds. Their lack of identity, encouraged by the short-sightedness of their ruling families and oil company sponsors, is a crippling malady which keeps them from becoming contributors to their countries.

While it is impossible to calculate a precise figure, most of the oil income of the past 40 years has gone into two things: the pockets of the ruling families and a small class of followers, and the purchase of arms the recipient countries can't use. Combined, these represent the most wasteful, profligate use of money history has seen.

King Fahd has 11 palaces; the one in Jeddah cost over US$5 billion. The Emir of Kuwait marries every Thursday; each wedding costs a small fortune. Sheikh Zayyed of Abu Dhabi entrusted his money to the founders of the Bank of Credit and Commerce International and had to pay US$3 billion to the bank's depositors on its collapse. The ruler of Qatar and his son conduct a royal family quarrel over a Swiss bank account with US$5 billion in it.

In the area of armament, Saudi Arabia has more fighter planes than pilots and more tanks than drivers as well as an elaborate electronic defence system its soldiers can't man. Kuwait spends billions arming a defence force of 30,000 which can't protect it against any invader. The United Arab Emirates recently bought 40 Mirage fighter-bombers from France, tripling the size of its air force at a stroke. And the rulers of Qatar are enamoured with building a navy, despite no obvious need to do so.

The attitude of the ruling families of these countries has resulted in a monopoly of power: the creation of a tiny class of supporters who don't relate to the problems of their countries and the squandering of their national wealth. All of which was supported by the oil companies and the governments that backed them. Committed to 'friends' — the rulers who guarantee the flow of oil at a 'reasonable price' — they have consistently subordinated the rights of the average Arab to these considerations. No western leader has ever spoken of human rights abuses in the oil-producing countries. The western media settles for superficial examination of conditions within these states and essentially follows its governments' official line. The small class of loyalists colludes in the distortion of the true conditions by sustaining the pretence that all is normal in their own countries.

But now, more than at any other time during this century, there are overwhelming reasons for the West to promote democracy and the consequent respect for human rights and the freedom of the press. Since the early 1980s there has been a considerable decline in oil income; the Middle Eastern oil-producing countries can no longer afford to bribe their people or western arms suppliers into silence. This serious economic downturn has taken place against a background of rising expectations and demands for democratic forms of government. Immediate steps must be taken to stop the use of oil as private income, the total monopoly of power and relegation of the common man to a nonentity. A crucial first step in forestalling the march towards disaster would be a cessation of the West's and oil companies' unqualified support for the ruling classes. Such progress could begin with the West serving notice on an elementary level: an unequivocal statement in support of democratic forces and freedom of expression in those countries which have been deprived of these by the alliance of western money and local self-interest. ❏

Saïd Aburish is a Palestinian writer living in London. His latest book, A Brutal Friendship: The West and the Arab Elite *was published by Gollancz in June*

OUTRAGE OR TIRED YAWN?

Large numbers of human rights reports are now issued and circulated every year. Many people devote their lives and even risk their personal safety to produce all this information.

But what happens next? Who sees all these reports? What effect does the information actually have: a sense of outrage which galvanises social action, or a tired yawn of recognition at seeing more of the same old stuff?

Human Rights Violations: Communicating Information is the outcome of an international workshop held in Oxford, 1995. This 52-page pamphlet with a report on the workshop by Stanley Cohen and articles by Ursula Owen, Caroline Moorehead, Rosemary Galang and Paddy Coulter, offers its readers provocative insight into the dilemmas facing human rights groups today.

HUMAN RIGHTS VIOLATIONS:
COMMUNICATING INFORMATION

discussion paper
from an
international workshop
Oxford 1995

'Human Rights Violations: Communicating Information' sells for £6 (US$10).

.... £/$........ enclosed for........ copies
Name
.... ❏ Cheque (UK£ or US$) ❏ Visa/MC/AmEx
Address
....
                                            Card no.
....
Postage is included.   Postcode   Expires

33 Islington High St, London N1 9LH   Tel: 44 171 278 2313   **INDEX**

BABEL

Colonos' complaint

La Pista, near Lago Agrio: balanced between oil men and Indians, no-one loves the colonos

UNTIL Texaco arrived to drill the first oil wells, the Oriente, Ecuador's Amazon jungle, was inaccessible; its indigenous people lived virtually undisturbed as they had for centuries. Oil pipelines brought roads however, and roads beckoned Ecuador's land-hungry poor from the Andes and the coastal plains beyond. Encouraged by the government's 'Living Frontiers' policy, these newcomers to the rainforest, the *colonos*, cut out thousands of acres of farms in the wake of the oil companies.

The invasion has been disastrous for the indigenous people of the Oriente, but the *colonos* too have suffered from building their homes next door to the oil wells. Blamed by all sides for destroying the jungle and creating a 'degenerate' society, they themselves confront devastating pollution from the very industry whose roads they followed.

Angel Olmedo Armijos is a colono *living on the Via Auca, the road that runs from Coca due south into the heart of Yasuni National Park. The father of five children, he moved to the area 12 years ago from the drought-stricken coastal province of Manabí.*

I WAS one of the founders of this village, Dayuma. I came from the coast like hundreds of others to cultivate a small farm and try to eke out a better existence. Ever since I arrived, however, companies have been coming to drill wells and extract oil and all the time they've been causing damage to the area and making our life harder. First they pollute the water, then the products that we grow and in the end the whole environment suffers. The contamination affects the fish particularly badly. My farm is over there by the lake where my children love to go fishing but sometimes, when there's a leakage, the oil spills onto the road, flows into the water and kills everything in it. Our animals drink from the river and the lake so some of them too have died. There have also been skin and intestinal problems among the people as we wash in the rivers and always use the water for cooking.

Crude is continuously seeping out, little by little, from the waste pits beside the wells. That well nearest to here, number 40, was drilled just six months ago and its waste pit has been left open. When it rains, the pit overflows and runs into the River Yumiyacu just below. The pit beside well number nine, which used to belong to Texaco, has been covered over with earth. Petroecuador is the main operator around here now and it has subcontracted other companies, including a Chinese one I think, to cover over many of the other pits in this way so that the people can't see them and don't complain. But they don't give the pits a real clean-up treatment: they just take out some of the waste and cover the rest with earth. So of

Shushuqui: living with oil — Credit: Emily Walmsley

course, when it's very hot, the oil bubbles up to the surface and when it rains the oil is washed down into the river.

There has been no control of these damages so we are continually denouncing them to the authorities, but they do nothing. First we used to tell Petroecuador, but that was no good, so now we tell Fundación Natura (a government ecological organisation) and INEFAN (a division of the Ministry of the Environment). They always say that they are going to do something, but in the end everything stays the same.

Celso Fernando Parra Granda, a 27-year-old colono, *lives in La Pista, a community on the outskirts of Lago Agrio, the first oil town in the Oriente. His arm was blown off 17 years ago by dynamite that Texaco had used for seismic exploration.*

Celso Fernando Parra Granda

IN 1980, when I was nine years old, I was walking home from school one day when I found some explosives by the side of the road. I didn't know what they were but like all children I was curious. I picked one up and started playing with it, knocking it around with sticks and things. Suddenly it exploded and my left arm was blown off.

The dynamite had been left lying around by Texaco who used it for seismic exploration. So they were responsible for my accident. In the first place, the company fitted me with a prosthetic arm, but afterwards they gave me nothing more, no money or anything to help my disability. I know that Texaco has my accident recorded because their doctor attended me, but later they said that there was no documentation of it. Then the company disappeared: it went back to its own country and there was no-one left from whom I could ask for help. I have lost many opportunities because of my arm. There are many activities, even in the day-to-day routine, that I find very difficult. In 1992 I asked Petroecuador to intervene in my case and speak to Texaco about giving me more compensation. But Petroecuador said it was Texaco's problem and they couldn't do anything about it.

All the people around here in Lago Agrio know about the explosives now. I was the example that warned everyone else: they saw what happened to me and they took more care. But until my accident happened, people used to decorate their houses with the bits of dynamite they found lying around, not knowing what they were. Just imagine, their houses could have been blown into a million little pieces. After my accident, experts were sent down from Quito with detectors and in the area of La Pista 5,000 more explosives were found within 10 centimetres of the surface. This is how irresponsible Texaco was: they never worried about the future generations of people who would come to colonise the area. When they worked here the company took no notice of the local people at all. At first we didn't realise how contaminated the place had become but when we tried to complain later, they said that the land belonged to them, that they had bought it from the Ecuadorian government, and so it was nothing to do with us.

At the moment I have work at the tree nursery of Petroecuador. The company put me in this department because I'm not much use working in other, more technical areas with only one real arm. I am also unable to help on the family farm much because of my disability. Basically, my future is very uncertain.

José Arnaldo Parra Camacho, Fernando's father, has a small farm on the outskirts of Lago Agrio. In recent years it has become drenched with toxic oil residues that have seeped through from the waste pit next to his land. In his late seventies, José depends on his farm for his livelihood.

I'VE had this farm for 16 years. I came here from the Colombian border and bought it, bit by bit, picking up pieces of land that other *colonos* had planted up then abandoned. The year that Texaco left, in 1992, I noticed that oil was seeping out of the earth in this corner here. It was coming from the waste pit next to the well just above the farm. Texaco covered it over with earth four years ago instead of getting rid of the crude elsewhere. Look, you can see clearly, just below the surface the soil is oozing crude.

At that time all this was planted with fruit trees. Little by little every one of them dried out and died as the oil contaminated the earth more and more. It's important to keep planting, however, because if I let the area become barren, the oil will spread further down towards the stream where my cattle drink. Some of my goats have already died from drinking polluted water. But there's no-one from whom I can claim compensation for their deaths.

As this waste pit was covered over by Texaco I went to ask them first to sort out the contamination on my land. They made lots of noise saying they would come and look tomorrow, the day after tomorrow, sometime soon; but they never appeared. People from Petroecuador came to see the problem but they just told me it was up to Texaco to do something about it. I haven't been able to talk to the men from Texaco since then because they've left the area and it's only me and my wife running this place so I can't leave to go and look for them. So you see, we haven't been able to do anything.

I come from Loja, in the southern Andes, originally. I went up to the Colombian border to look for land for a farm after serving in the army for 25 years — I fought in the war against Peru in 1942. But the Colombians wanted to kill me and I was scared that my children would become orphans so we moved down here. I have five sons and I wanted them to study so that they could work for the company. There was no village then where Lago Agrio is now. It was all wild and only 10 kilometres from here into the jungle you wouldn't find a soul. Texaco began to fill up the area, bringing materials to build more roads, and that's how the town grew.

When we first arrived I got a job with Texaco looking after the wells. There wasn't much machinery at that time so we had to direct the oil coming up from the wells manually into the pumps so that it would flow down the pipeline. The company treated me well throughout the 15 years I was employed by them. I feel very humble to have worked with those men — we never argued once. Since Texaco left, however, they've modernised the equipment and people aren't needed to look after the wells any more.

These days I work mainly on the farm: we live from its produce. Now that it is so polluted I would like to sell up and buy some more land farther into the jungle. But in reality no-one's going to buy this farm from me now — it's not worth anything full of oil — and I'm too old to go trekking off into the forest. I just hope that one day the company realises what it has done and comes back to help me. ❑

Interviews by Emily Walmsley

THE **INDEX** READERS

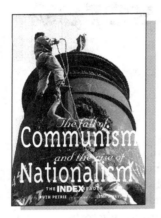 

Communism and Nationalism

Václav Havel, Andrei Sakharov, Salman Rushdie, Geoffrey Hosking, Dubravka Ugresic, Adam Michnik and many others bear witness to the crumbling of the Communist empire in Europe and its transformation into fledgling democracies or nationalist regimes.

The Fall of Communism and the Rise of Nationalism includes essays from the first 25 years of Index to portray the complex reality of the Communist world and its collapse in Europe.

Film and Censorship

Film-makers, critics and academics from around the world explore why film has been perceived to be a dangerous medium.

James Ivory, Andrej Wajda, Roman Polanski, Tony Rayns, Pedro Almódovar, Philip French, Milos Forman, Arthur C Clark and others bring into sharp focus the many different ways in which film is censored—from the obvious banning and cutting to hidden methods of suppression such as self-censorship and refusals of funding.

Each INDEX reader sells for £10—subscribers save £3 off the bookshop price.

Enter my order for ❏ Communism and Nationalism
❏ Film and Censorship

....
Name

....

....

................................/...............................
Postcode

£/$........ enclosed for...... readers
Outside of the UK, please pay £12 ($18) per reader.

❏ Cheque (UK£ or US$)   ❏ Visa/MC/AmEx

....
Card no.

....
Expires

....
Signature

INDEX, 33 Islington High St, London N1 9LH Tel: 44 171 278 2313

EDWARD LUCIE-SMITH

On being censored

Art falls foul of a peculiarly British taboo

IT'S AN odd sensation: writing against censorship fairly frequently, then being censored oneself. The occasion? A new book of mine, *Ars Erotica*, is due shortly from a pair of very reputable publishers, one on either side of the Atlantic. The text is written, the illustrations chosen, the page layouts done. Suddenly the British publisher begins to agitate: he has been consulting his lawyers, and the lawyers are not happy. The problem is — er — largely the number of erections in the book. Photographic erections that is. Where paintings and drawings are concerned you can now print almost anything you like — though the further into the past you go the better. Group buggery on a Greek pot, for example, is perfectly OK. As it happens, I haven't chosen that particular illustration, largely because it has been so much published already.

But photographs — 'photographs less than 50 years old' — that's another matter altogether. There are a number of illustrations in the book which, it transpires, contravene two powerful taboos. The first is connected with the magic power of the camera. Though everyone now knows how easily, in the digital age, photographs can be altered or faked — that is, we accept, at least intellectually, that they can be as much 'fictions' as things which are drawn or painted — we still have a visceral reaction to them. Other forms of visual representation we see as acts of the imagination, even when we are told that the artist actually sat down before the event represented and scrutinised it thoroughly. But photographs! These seem to assure us that the erotic event in question actually took place, in the presence of a witness, and it is that that somehow disturbs the good order of society.

The other taboo is more peculiarly British: the erect penis, indeed even the *suggestion* or the *possibility* of an erect penis, makes even perfectly sensible people in this country go all wobbly (quite the opposite in fact of the penis itself). The Japanese feel the same about female pubic hair, but nevertheless publish some of the most extravagant erotica in the world.

There has just been a delightful example of this British foible in the world of television advertising. A new TV commercial shows a girl who, we are assured, is wearing a perfume called Impulse. She walks into a class of artists painting a nude male model. The model notices her perfume and reacts. Though the actual physical result of his reaction is not shown, his expressions and body language make it quite clear what is happening. The result was immediately denounced by some self-appointed keeper of public morals as 'leading to cultural degeneration'. The phrase itself, of course, carries its own cultural echo.

Where my book was concerned, once the lawyers' protest had been made, a phase of negotiation began. How many erections could we save? Here is one, for instance, which first made its appearance in a book published in Britain in 1991 and which has been continuously in print ever since. Here is another: a new shot of a model whose likeness, with an even more impressive hard-on, appeared in another book published in Britain in 1995. Both books have been regularly sold in large general bookstores. No legal problems have ensued. Can we use those? No. Those were books addressed to a 'specialist' (read 'homosexual') audience. *Ars Erotica* is intended for the general public, and deals with a wide range of sexualities.

But *this* erection (the largest and most prominent of them all) is probably OK. The reason is that, while it looks more like a shot borrowed from a gay erotic magazine than any of the others, it is in fact the work of a celebrated American artist — none other than Andres Serrano, whose *Piss Christ* aroused controversy some time back (see *Index* 3/1996). Since then Serrano has gone up in the world: his work featured in the last Venice Biennale. The image chosen for my book was commissioned by a Dutch museum (the innovative Groninger Museum in Groningen) for its own permanent collection, and the transparency was supplied by them. If you are famous enough and official enough, the situation changes. You can probably depict what you like, even if you insist on using a camera to do it. Jeff Koons, after all, got away with explicit photographic scenes of coitus, not merely on the walls of art galleries, but in a couple of widely distributed books (see *Index* 2/1995).

In addition to the offending photographs, there is just one painting the British publisher is dying to get rid of. It shows *The Flagellation* and is from a series of Stations of the Cross by the New Mexican artist Delmas Howe (who is represented in the British Museum and also in the Fitzwilliam Museum, Cambridge). The composition is very close to traditional versions of the subject — there is a resemblance to a famous Flagellation by the seventeenth century Bolognese painter Ludovico Carracci, which is even more violent, with the participants almost equally unclad. But in Howe's work the figures are wearing leather trappings which identify them as members of the modern gay S&M community. The connection between pain, pleasure and religious feeling is openly spelt out.

But there is another layer of irony, made even more ironic by the attempt to suppress the image. The Christ in Delmas Howe's Passion scene is a highly recognisable portrait — yes, I have met the model — of a man who, very recently, after a long lawsuit, received a six-figure settlement from the Roman Catholic diocese of Albuquerque as compensation for sexual abuse suffered at the hands of its priests when he was a child.

So far Howe's *Flagellation* is still in my book — at least as far as I know. But watch this space. ❑

Edward Lucie-Smith *is a poet, writer and art critic. His most recent book is* ArToday (Phaidon, 1996)

BANNED — 'Mike Welder' by Jack Fritscher

SAVED BY FAME — A History of Sex, 1996 by Andres Serrano
Credit: The Groninger Museum, Netherlands

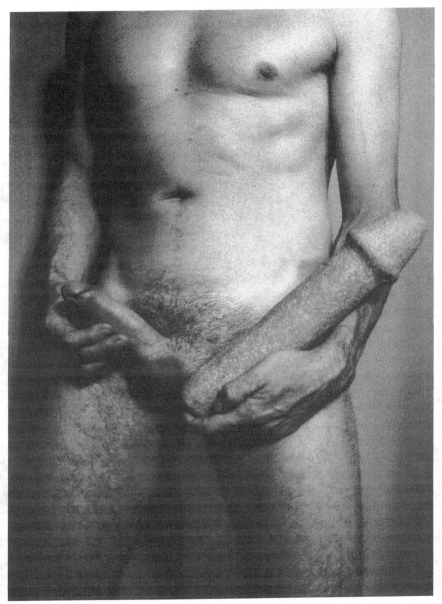

LAST MOMENT REPRIEVE — Untitled 1996 by Edward Lucie-Smith

UNDER THREAT — The Flagellation (Stations) Study, 1997 by Delmas Howe

SAVED BY ITS AGE — *Flagellation of Christ by Ludovico Carracci*
Credit: Musée de la Chartreuse, Douai, Giraudon

DIARY

ADAM NEWEY

Fujimori's 15 minutes

Lima, Peru: aboard the colectivo: — *Credit: Victor Bustamante/TAFOS/Panos Pictures*

Friday, 9 May

WE arrive mid-evening, exhausted after 18 hours on the wing via Amsterdam and Aruba. Although it's well into autumn here it feels sticky and stifling after the London spring we've left behind.

On the way in from the airport, Lima seems like one big snarl of cars, taxis and buses, everyone making their way home at the end of the week. Our driver weaves through what gaps there are in the traffic, making heavy use of the horn. To pass the time, his mate asks us where we're from, how long we're here, whether it's our first time in Peru — all the usual things you ask tourists. I tell him we're here partly on business, that we work for a magazine.

'Ah, journalists,' he says. 'Of course, you're here to cover the visit of Mr Hashimoto.' Before I can put him right he explains that during the siege the Japanese Embassy became a regular stop on the taxi driver's itinerary. It was the one place that every foreign journalist wanted to see. 'That,' he adds as if to emphasise the point, 'was a big story.' Peru doesn't generate many big news stories, and we've arrived just as this one is winding up. Mr Hashimoto, I assume, is here to tie up any loose ends.

I remember being rather surprised to read that the ambassador, far from being welcomed back, has been sent home in total disgrace. I'm also surprised to hear that there is near-universal acclaim for the way the siege was broken. President Fujimori's approval rating doubled overnight, and no-one seems at all interested in whether the hostage-takers were killed in battle, or shot in cold blood while trying to surrender, as some of their captives claimed. Anyway, what's the difference? The outcome is the same whichever way you slice it.

Saturday, 10 May

DAYLIGHT reveals Lima to be bigger, busier, noisier and more crowded even than it seemed last night. For now we've opted to ignore the flashy modern suburb of Miraflores, where most of the tourists go, in favour of the old city centre. Here the narrow streets are sclerotic with traffic, most of them buses and taxis, horns blaring, looking for passengers; while the precincts and plazas are crowded with shoeshine boys, money changers, barrows piled high with *churros* and other confections, old women offering to tell you your weight, street vendors hawking tools, combs and racks of clothes, small, dusty-looking children clutching boxes of gum — there are people everywhere and everyone is touting for business. And the smell is overpowering — a decoction of broiled chicken, bad drains and heavily leaded exhaust fumes.

We head up towards the Plaza de Armas, which is where the presidential palace is. This has been the seat of almost absolute power since Fujimori's 'self-coup' of 1992. (He was already president. His coup consisted in cutting Congress out of the picture and suspending the Constitution. Both have since been restored, but in a politically neutered form.) The plaza also marks the spot where, in 1535, the great conquistador Francisco Pizarro took out his sword, cut a cross in the desert sand and sketched out the gridplan of his new city, which became the capital of the Spanish viceroyalty. It's hard to equate that elegant colonial town with today's sprawling megalopolis, though strong traces certainly remain.

As we enter the square, it's clear there's something going on. Armed police are keeping the crowds in check. It's hard to put your finger on, but there's a sullenness, a feeling of suppressed resentment in the air. The police are clearing the centre of the square and everyone is herding round the sides, beneath the arcades and porticoes. We push through the crowd towards the palace, just in time to see a motorcade sweep out of the gates and away round the corner. Nearby I can see a couple of men holding crude placards saying 'Welcome Mr Hashimoto' and 'Viva Japan'. But they look bored and listless, as if they don't really mean it.

Even though the cars have gone the police still won't let us walk round in front of the palace, so we walk round the back instead. Right behind the palace is the river Rimac. Now, at the end of the summer, it's barely a trickle, its bed littered with rubbish. On the far side the shanty towns spread out and up into the sand dunes, while on this side an armoured car, topped with a water cannon, is driving slowly around and sweeping away the stallholders and marketeers that gather along the embankment. It's done in a desultory kind of way, with the water turned down low. Perhaps they don't really mean it either. Nevertheless, it's another small reminder that violence, or the threat of it, is what underwrites the exercise of power here.

★ ★ ★

Sunday, 11 May

A N URGE to get out of the city leads us to head for Pachacamac, a pre-Inca citadel overlooking the ocean 20 miles to the south, originally dedicated to the god of earthquakes. Given the number of times Lima has been devastated by earthquakes and landslips, he evidently takes some appeasing.

We haul ourselves aboard a *colectivo*, which grinds a laborious path through some of the dirt-poor areas to the southeast, where the road is fringed with grubby barrows selling fruit and vegetables, and mountains of urban refuse rise up hard by. These buses don't have regular stops. Rather, they skirt the pavement while the conductor leans out of the side door, yelling the names of places along the route and trying to scoop up would-be passengers. They barely come to a halt at all. Our conductor is a typical mestizo, lean and smooth-looking, with high cheekbones, aquiline nose and thick, jet-black hair. He's expert at his job, leaping in and out, risking his neck to ensure the bus is packed to the rafters, shooing people off — 'bajo, 'bajo — and pulling others on. The guidebook cheerfully points out that these buses have a dismal safety record.

After a while the highway widens into a major concrete artery pumping traffic and fumes out of the city. Away to the left I notice a small, ramshackle sign pointing along a narrow road that winds up to the shanties in the hills. It says 'Villa El Salvador'. I recognise the name because it's the place where María Elena Moyano was murdered.

Moyano led a powerful grassroot women's movement in the town a few years ago. She was young, popular and an outspoken critic of Sendero Luminoso, who were then very active in the area. The government was doing nothing for the poor but Moyano offered the poor a chance of doing something to help themselves. They elected her deputy mayor, at the age of just 31. It was an overwhelming vote for change without violence. But Sendero, being dogmatically opposed to 'reformism' — especially feminist reformism — couldn't countenance such a challenge to their authority. They reckon it false consciousness to think that any kind of social justice can be established in the current order. And since the revolution requires sacrifices even of the poorest, they machine-gunned Moyano down in front of her supporters, and her children, then strapped dynamite to her body and blew her to pieces. The logic of terrorism is relentless. Sendero's strategy was to give these people the starkest of choices, between a life of hopeless poverty and the hope, however illusory, of justice through bloodshed. Hardly surprising if some of them opt for the latter.

Thursday, 15 May

IN THE middle of this, an international conference on freedom of expression offers a strange set of contrasts. It's being held at a smart hotel/convention centre about half an hour east of the city, surrounded by the sprawl of *pueblos jóvenes* ('young towns'). We are warned not to leave the hotel compound. These self-built shanty towns really are desperate places, teetering up the side of the desert hills, with practically nothing in the way of basic utilities. They'd stand up no better than a house of cards if an earthquake struck. Judging from the frame poles that are left sticking out of the top of them, many of the buildings are intended to grow higher than their single storey, but people move in as soon as the ground floor has a ceiling on it. This gives the towns a permanent building-site feel, compared with the relatively genteel dilapidation that characterises central Lima.

The road that leads out of town is lined with places selling rough bricks, mortar, corrugated iron roofing — everything you need to build your own shack. Fujimori's economic shock therapy may have succeeded in curbing Peru's hyperinflation, but there's precious little trickling down to the majority who live out here. No wonder everyone is hustling for a buck in downtown Lima. And the *pueblos* continue to suck in the rural poor, accounting for Lima's spectacular growth, from three million in the 1970s to over eight million people today.

There's a rumour that Sendero set off a huge car-bomb last night about a mile from here. Safe in our compound we heard nothing, and papers are hard to come by, but assuming it's true it would appear that Sendero are determined to re-establish themselves as Peru's premier terror group, now that the MRTA have had their 15 minutes of fame.

Saturday, 17 May

There have been a couple of real highlights to the conference. One was a talk by Jesús Alfonso Castiglione Mendoza, a radio journalist who was sentenced to 20 years for his putative links with Sendero. Incredibly, the case against him was built solely on the fact that he once rented an apartment which was later used by a Sendero cell planning a prison breakout. This is a fairly typical outcome of the faceless court system, which has led to dozens of miscarriages of justice. A systematic review of these cases began last year, but was suspended during the embassy siege and hasn't yet got under way again. Although Castiglione has been out for a few months now, he still wears that slightly shrunken,

Jesús Alfonso Castiglione Mendoza

spooked look you often see in ex-prisoners. Very gravely he gives us each a gift to thank us for our efforts on his case, which is profoundly touching.

The other high point was meeting Enrique Zileri, the editor of *Caretas* magazine and one of my heroes. Zileri really stuck his neck out at the height of the repression after the 1992 coup, when everything was geared to the fight against terrorism, by investigating Fujimori's shadowy security adviser, Vladimiro Montesinos. Last night we went for a drink at the magazine's offices overlooking the Plaza de Armas. It was a warm evening and we stood on the balcony looking over the square, Zileri talking about what it was like for journalists when Lima was a place of real terror and they had to keep out of view as far as they could. Now that things are a little safer again they want to be able to keep a close eye on what's going on. Hence the decision to move the offices here, to the centre of power, directly opposite the presidential palace, with the cathedral to the right and Lima city hall to the left. It seems highly appropriate that the fourth side of the square should be devoted to the press.

Wednesday, 21 May

A FTER a couple of days in the mountains, it's time to head home. Our last few hours are spent catching up on museums. Driving through the suburbs, our taxi driver strikes up the usual tourist conversation. Like almost everyone else we've met here, he wants to talk about the siege; and like almost everyone else, he's full of patriotic pride for the way it ended. 'Wasn't that great, the way they dealt with the terrorists?' he enthuses, assuming assent. 'That really showed them!'

He talks a little about his house in one of the quieter suburbs, not far from the museum we're going to. His car is one of the fleet of brand new shiny Hyundais, which are taking over from the rusting Beetles that used to be the taxi driver's vehicle of choice. From this I guess that he's done reasonably well out of the Fujimori years. A little later, as we're driving past one of the universities, he tells us how the authorities showed similar grit in rooting out Sendero sympathisers — or suspected sympathisers — there as well. He mimes gunfire to make sure I know what he means. Whether he means it literally, I don't know, but it doesn't make much difference. For him this has nothing to do with notions of right or justice or law; it's simply a price worth paying, or no price at all, for the guarantee of stability and a chance to make a decent living wage. ❏

Adam Newey, *formerly* Index's *news editor, has recently joined the* New Statesman

★ ★ ★